Introduction

A: Legal and management

B: Health and welfare

C: General safety

D: High risk activities

E: Environment

D1382054

Contents

F: Specialist activities

The following specialist activities are included within the managers and professionals test and **all** need to be revised.

Further information

Introduction

Contents

Foreword

The construction industry will always be inherently dangerous for people working on site. It is the way we recognise and manage that risk which makes a difference to them.

The role of managers and professionals in helping to recognise and manage risk and so raise health and safety standards is significant and, until recently, underestimated (whether they are architects, engineers, site managers, quantity surveyors or one of the many other disciplines involved in the design, procurement and construction process).

The CITB *Health, safety and environment test for managers and professionals* continues to give managers and professionals essential health, safety and environmental knowledge. This has an enormous influence, not just on the construction techniques used, but also on the values and ethos of the sites themselves.

Managing health, safety and the environment is not about policing. It concerns behaviour and the broad and deep consensus that unsafe sites or uncontrolled activities with the potential to damage the environment are unacceptable in any circumstances. This is a responsibility placed on all of us.

As professionals, we need to show leadership by example and not be escorted visitors on our own sites. Obtaining the correct card is a clear sign that a fully trained workforce is key.

We have a great industry. However, it must become a healthier and safer one for all those that work in it. It must also take its environmental responsibilities seriously for the sake of future generations.

Graham Watts OBE

Chief Executive
Construction Industry Council

About the test

The CITB *Health, safety and environment test* helps raise standards across the industry. It ensures that workers at all levels meet a minimum level of health, safety and environmental awareness before going on site. It should be used as a stepping stone, encouraging employers, managers and professionals, and their workforce to go on and develop their knowledge even further.

Preparing for a test

To pass your *Health, safety and environment test* you need to demonstrate knowledge and understanding across a number of areas, all of which are relevant to people working in a construction environment. There is not a minimum pass mark, but sectional scoring, with minimum scores allocated to each section. This test structure has been designed to enable you to demonstrate knowledge across all of these key areas.

The knowledge questions are grouped in chapters and sections, following the same structure that is used in all core CITB publications.

Section A: Legal and management

Section B: Health and welfare

Section C: General safety

Section D: High risk activities

Section E: Environment

Section F: Specialist activities

Section A: Legal and management

General responsibilities: what you and your employer need to do to ensure everyone is working safely on site.

Accident reporting and recording: when, how and why accidents need to be reported and recorded.

Section B: Health and welfare

Health and welfare: common health issues on site and how to avoid them. Providing welfare facilities and support on site.

First aid and emergency procedures: what you should do in case of an emergency, and what your employer must make available.

Personal protective equipment: why personal protective equipment (PPE) is important, why you should wear it and who is responsible for it.

Dust and fumes (respiratory hazards): how to work safely, protecting yourself and those around you from exposure to respiratory hazards. What health conditions may arise from exposure to dust and fumes.

Noise and vibration: why it is important to minimise exposure to noise and vibration in the work place. How you should protect yourself and those around you.

Hazardous substances: how you can identify a hazardous substance, and what control measures should be in place to enable you to work safely.

Manual handling: why and how it is important to handle all loads using a safe system of work. What key areas you need to be aware of when handling loads.

Section C: General safety

Safety signs: what type of safety signs you will see on a construction site, and what they are informing you of.

Fire prevention and control: what you should do if you discover a fire, and which fire extinguishers should be used on what type of fire.

Electrical safety, tools and equipment: how to work with different types of tools safely, and what you should do if the tools you are using have not been examined or are faulty.

Site transport safety and lifting operations: how site vehicles and pedestrians should work together on site.

Section D: High risk activities

Working at height: what types of equipment you will use working at height, and how to use them correctly.

Excavations and confined spaces: why it is important, and how, to work safely in a confined space or excavation, and what you should do if exposed to certain hazards.

Section E: Environment

Environmental awareness and waste control: your responsibilities on site, how waste should be managed and how to conserve energy.

Section F: Specialist activities

You will also be asked questions from the three specialist activities which are Construction (Design and Management) Regulations, Demolition, and Highway works.

How is the test structured?

All tests last for 45 minutes and have 50 multiple-choice questions. There are two different types of question, behavioural case study questions and knowledge questions.

What is a behavioural case study question?

The behavioural case study questions are designed to test how you respond to health and safety situations on a construction site.

Three case studies are included in your test, each of which has four linked multiple-choice questions.

The questions progress through a fictional situation faced by an individual working in the construction industry. They are based on the principles established in the film *Setting out* – what you should expect from a site and what they expect from you.

Further information on the film and the transcript is provided at the back of this book.

What is a knowledge question?

The knowledge questions cover 19 core areas (presented in Sections A-F of this book) that are included in all the tests. These questions are very factual. For example they will ask you to identify fire extinguishers and signs.

You will not need a detailed knowledge of the exact content or working of any regulations. However, you will need to show that you know what is required of you, the things you must do (or not do), and what to do in certain circumstances (for example, when you, or one of your workers discovers an accident).

Many of the questions refer to the duties of employers. In law, the self-employed can have the same legal responsibilities as employers. To keep the questions as brief as possible, the content only refers to the duties of employers but the questions apply to both.

Legislation in Northern Ireland and Scotland differs from that in the rest of the UK. For practical reasons, all candidates (including those in Northern Ireland and Scotland) will be tested on questions using legislation relevant to the remainder of the UK only.

Who writes the questions?

The question bank is developed by CITB with industry-recognised organisations which sit on or support the Health, safety and environment test question sub-committee. A full list of those parties that support the test is set out in the acknowledgements at the back of the book.

Will the questions change?

Health, safety and environment legislation, regulations and best practice will change from time to time, but CITB makes every effort to keep the test and the revision material up to date.

- You will not be tested on questions that are deemed to no longer be appropriate.

- You will be tested on knowledge questions presented in the most up to date edition of the book. To revise effectively for the test you should use the latest edition. You can check which edition of the book you have at www.citb.co.uk/hsandetestupdate or phone 0344 994 4488.

There are a number of ways you can prepare for your test.

	Operatives	Specialists	Supervisors	Managers
Watch *Setting out*	Free to view at *www.citb.co.uk/settingout*			
Read the question and answer books	HS&E test for operatives and specialists (GT 100)			HS&E test for managers and professionals – (GT 200)
Use the digital products	HS&E test for operatives and specialists – DVD (GT 100 DVD) – Download (GT 100 DL) – App			HS&E test for managers and professionals – DVD (GT 200 DVD) – Download (GT 200 DL) – App
Read supporting knowledge material	Safe start (GE 707)	Safe start (GE 707) plus sector recommended supporting material	Site supervision simplified (GE 706)	Construction site safety (GE 700)
Complete an appropriate training course	Site Safety Plus – one-day Health and safety awareness course	Contact your industry body for recommendations	Site Safety Plus – two-day Site supervisor's safety training scheme	Site Safety Plus – five-day Site management safety training scheme

How can I increase my chances of success?

☑ Prepare using the recommended revision materials, working through all the knowledge questions.

☑ Watch the *Setting out* film to prepare for the behavioural case study questions.

☑ Complete a recommended training course.

☑ Book your test when you are confident with your topics and questions.

☑ Complete a timed simulated test, which is available on the DVD, app and download.

What's on the DVD, app and download?

The DVD, app and download offer an interactive package that includes:

☑ the *Setting out* film and a sample behavioural case study

☑ all the knowledge questions and answers in both book and practice formats

☑ a test simulator – all the functionality of the test with the real question bank

☑ voice-overs in English and Welsh for all questions.

Where can I buy the revision material?

CITB has developed a range of revision material, including question and answer books, DVDs, downloads and a smartphone app that will help you to prepare for the test. For further information and to buy these products:

@ go online at *www.citb.co.uk/hsanderevision*

📞 telephone 0344 994 4488

ℹ️ visit a good bookshop, either in the high street or online for books and DVDs. Visit iTunes or Google Play for smartphone apps.

Where can I find more information on your supporting publications?

CITB has developed a range of publications that present a detailed and comprehensive guide to the full range of topics covered in the test. They can be used to build awareness and understanding of the issues surrounding health and safety on a construction site. They provide the context for the questions that are asked.

The range of products includes: *Safe start* (GE 707), *Site supervision simplified* (GE 706) and *Construction site safety* (GE 700). For further information and to buy these products:

 go online at *http://shop.citb.co.uk*

 telephone 0344 994 4122
lines open Monday to Thursday 9am to 5pm and Friday 9am to 4pm.

What is the Site Safety Plus Scheme?

The Site Safety Plus scheme provides a number of courses that will enhance and develop your skills within the building, civil engineering and allied industries.

Courses give everyone, from operative to senior manager, the skills they need to progress.

For further information:

 go online at *www.citb.co.uk/training-and-courses/site-safety-plus*

Booking a test

The easiest way to book your test is either online or by telephone. You will be given the date and time of your test immediately and offered the opportunity to buy revision material (for example a book, DVD, download or app). You should be able to book a test at your preferred location within two weeks.

To book your test:

 go online at *www.citb.co.uk/hsandetest*

 telephone 0344 994 4488

 post in an application form (application forms are available from the website and the telephone number listed above).

When booking your test you will be able to choose whether to receive confirmation by email or by letter. It is important that you check the details (including the type of test, the location, the date and time) and follow any instructions it gives regarding the test.

You can also choose to receive an SMS text message or email reminder 24 hours before your test.

For those instances where a test is required at short notice it may be possible to turn up at a centre and take a test on the day (subject to available spaces). It's strongly advised that you do not rely on this option.

If you do not receive a confirmation email or letter within the time specified please call the booking line to check your booking has been made.

We cannot take responsibility for postal delays. If you miss your test event, you will unfortunately forfeit your fee.

What information do I need to book a test?

To book a test you should have the following information to hand.

- Which test you need to take.
- Whether you require any special assistance.
- Your chosen method of payment (debit or credit card details).
- Your address details.
- Your CITB registration number (you will have one of these if you have taken the test before, or applied for certain card schemes including CSCS, CPCS, CISRS, etc.).

Where can I take a test?

To sit a *Health, safety and environment test* you will need to visit a CITB-approved test centre. There are three different types of centre.

- **Fixed test centres.** These are operated by our delivery provider. To find your nearest test centre visit *www.citb.co.uk/hsandetest*. These test centres will be able to offer tests from Monday to Saturday, but local opening times will vary. Normal opening hours are Monday to Friday 8am to 8pm and Saturday 8am to noon.
- **Independent test centres.** These would include those operated by a college, training provider or commercial organisation. Please contact these test centres directly for further information and to book a test.
- **Mobile testing services.** These can be established at a suitable venue for a group of candidates. For further information on this service there is a dedicated booking line 0344 994 4492.

All CITB-approved test centres charge the same price for a *Health, safety and environment test*. For information regarding the cost of a test:

@ go online at *www.citb.co.uk/cards-testing/health-safety-environment-test*

Is there any special assistance available when taking the test?

Voice-over assistance

All tests can be booked with English or Welsh voice-overs.

Foreign language assistance

- The managers and professionals test does not allow foreign language assistance because a basic command of English or Welsh is required in order to sit the test.
- The operatives test can be booked with voice-overs in the following languages: Bulgarian, Czech, French, German, Hungarian, Lithuanian, Polish, Portuguese, Punjabi, Romanian, Russian, Spanish.

  An interpreter can be requested if assistance is required in other languages.
- The specialist tests can be booked with an interpreter but no pre-recorded voice-overs are available.

Sign language assistance

The operatives test can be booked with British Sign Language on screen. If you need assistance in the other tests a signer can be provided.

What services are there for Welsh speakers?

- All tests can be booked with Welsh voice-overs.
- All revision DVDs include Welsh voice-overs.
- There is a dedicated Welsh booking line 0344 994 4490.

How do I cancel or postpone my test?

To cancel or reschedule your test you should go online or call the booking number at least 72 hours (three working days) before your test. There will be no charge for cancelling or rescheduling the test online at www.citb.co.uk/testingservices outside of the 72 hour period. Reschedules and cancellations made via the telephone booking line will incur an administration fee.

Taking a test

Before the test

On the day of the test you will need to:

- allow plenty of time to get to the test centre and arrive at least 15 minutes before the start of the test
- take your confirmation email or letter
- take proof of identity that bears your photo and your signature (such as driving licence card or passport – please visit *www.citb.co.uk/hsandetest* for full list of acceptable documentation).

On arrival at the test centre, staff will check your documents to ensure you are booked onto the correct test. If you do not have all the relevant documents you will not be able to sit your test and you will lose your fee.

During the test

The tests are all delivered on a computer screen. However, you do not need to be familiar with computers and the test does not involve any typing. All you need to do is click on the relevant answer boxes, using either a mouse or by touching the screen.

Before the test begins you can choose to work through a tutorial. It explains how the test works and lets you try out the buttons and functions that you will use while taking your test.

There will be information displayed on the screen which shows you how far you are through the test and how much time you have remaining.

After the test

At the end of the test there is an optional survey that gives you the chance to provide feedback on the test process.

You will be provided with a printed score report after you have left the test room. This will tell you whether you have passed or failed your test, and give feedback on areas where further learning and revision is recommended.

What do I do if I fail?

If you fail your test, your score report will provide feedback on areas where you got questions wrong.

It is strongly recommended that you revise these areas thoroughly before re-booking. You will have to wait at least 48 hours before you can take the test again.

What do I do if I pass?

A *Health, safety and environment test* pass is often a necessary requirement when applying to join a construction industry card scheme. Different schemes exist in different trades and professions. Membership of a relevant scheme helps you prove that you can do your job, and that you can do it safely. Access to construction sites may require a relevant scheme card.

Once you have passed your test, you should, if you have not done so already, consider applying to join the relevant card scheme. However please be aware that you may need to complete further training, assessment and/or testing to meet their specific entry requirements.

To find out more about many of the recognised schemes:

@ go online at *www.citb.co.uk/cardschemes.*

Further scheme contact details		telephone	go online
General	Construction Skills Certification Scheme (CSCS)	0344 994 4777	www.cscs.uk.com
	Northern Ireland: Construction Skills Register (CSR)	028 9087 7150	www.cefni.co.uk
Plant operatives	Construction Plant Competence Scheme (CPCS)	0844 815 7274	www.citb.co.uk/cpcs
Scaffolders	Construction Industry Scaffolders Record Scheme (CISRS)	0844 815 7223	www.cisrs.org.uk
HVACR	Engineering Services SKILLcard (ESS)	01768 860 406	www.skillcard.org.uk
Plumbers	Joint Industry Board for Plumbing and Mechanical Engineering Services (JIB-PMES)	01480 476 925	www.jib-pmes.org
	Scottish and Northern Ireland Joint Industry Board (SNJIB)	0131 556 0600	www.ecscard.org.uk

Fraudulent testing

CITB takes reports of fraud linked to our testing processes extremely seriously. Working with the Police and other law enforcement agencies, we are doing everything we can to address the issue. Where possible, we always prosecute those engaged in any fraudulent activity.

If you are aware of any fraudulent activity in the delivery of your test, or relating to cards or training in the construction industry:

 email our fraud investigation team on *report.it@citb.co.uk*

Augmented reality

What is augmented reality?

Augmented reality (AR) technology is used in our publications to provide readers with additional digital content such as videos, images and web-links.

This technology has been used to connect you with extra, complementary content. This can be accessed via your mobile device using the Layar app.

> **[!] How to install and use the Layar app**
>
> ☑ Go to the appropriate app store (Apple or Android) and download the Layar app (free of charge) to your mobile device.
> ☑ Look out for the AR logo (right), which indicates a Layar-friendly page or image.
> ☑ Open the Layar app and scan the Layar-friendly page or image (ensure that you have the whole page or the specific image in view whilst scanning).
> ☑ Wait for the page to activate on your device.
> ☑ Select one of the buttons that have appeared to access the additional content.

Where can I find augmented reality in this publication?

The following content is accessible by scanning the cover page of this publication.

☑ Book a *Health, safety and environment test*.

☑ Watch the *Setting out* film.

☑ Buy revision material.

☑ Buy the *Health, safety and environment test* revision app (Apple and Android).

☑ Buy supporting publications.

A

Legal and management

Contents

01 General responsibilities

1.01

Why is the Health and Safety at Work Act important to everyone at work? Give **two** answers.

- [A] It explains how health and safety is managed on site
- [B] It explains how to write risk assessments
- [C] It requires all employers to provide a safe place to work
- [D] It sets out how work should be carried out
- [E] It puts legal duties on workers with regard to their acts or omissions

1.02

Why should all employees be able to view the company health and safety policy?

- [A] It tells them how to do their job safely
- [B] It contains the contents of the risk assessments
- [C] It tells them how health and safety is managed within their organisation
- [D] It tells them how to use tools and equipment safely

1.03

If there is a fatal accident or reportable dangerous occurrence on site, when **must** the Health and Safety Executive (HSE) be informed?

- [A] Immediately
- [B] Within five days
- [C] Within seven days
- [D] Within ten days

1.04

What happens if a prohibition notice is issued by a Health and Safety Executive (HSE) inspector or Local Authority?

- [A] Work can continue, as long as a risk assessment is carried out
- [B] The work that is subject to the notice must stop
- [C] Work can continue if extra safety precautions are taken
- [D] The work currently in progress can be completed, but no new work can be started

Answers: 1.01 = C, E   1.02 = C   1.03 = A   1.04 = B

**A
01**

1.05

A whole site has been issued with a prohibition notice. What does this mean during the period that the notice applies?

- A You must be on site before work starts
- B The site manager must check with the Health and Safety Executive (HSE) before starting work
- C No-one must use any survey equipment, tools or machinery
- D All work must stop on site until the safety problem is rectified

1.06

When does an employer have to prepare a written health and safety policy and record the significant findings of risk assessments?

- A When they employ three or more people
- B When they employ five or more people
- C When they employ 10 or more people
- D When the work is going to last for more than 30 days

1.07

In the context of a risk assessment, what does the term **risk** mean?

- A Something with the potential to cause injury
- B An unsafe act or condition
- C The likelihood or chance that a hazard could actually cause harm or damage
- D Any work activity that can be described as dangerous

1.08

What does a risk assessment tell you?

- A How significant risks are being created
- B What legislation should be applied to control risks
- C The generic risks associated with an activity
- D What risks may exist and how they should be controlled

1.09

The significant findings of a risk assessment reveal a risk to health or safety of site staff. What measure should always be considered **first**?

- A Make sure personal protective equipment (PPE) is available
- B Adapt the work to the individual
- C Give priority to those measures that protect the whole workforce
- D Avoid the risk altogether if possible

Answers: 1.05 = D   1.06 = B   1.07 = C   1.08 = D   1.09 = D

General responsibilities

1.10

What is the purpose of an on-site risk assessment?

A) To save time completing documentation

B) To review hazards and risks to ensure that any planned safety system is still applicable

C) To ensure that the work can be carried out in a reasonable timeframe

D) To protect the company from prosecution

1.11

In considering what measures to take to protect workers against risks to their health and safety, when should personal protective equipment (PPE) be considered?

A) First, because it is an effective way to protect people

B) First, as the only practical measure

C) Never, as using PPE is bad practice

D) Only when the risks cannot be eliminated by other means

1.12

What does the word hazard mean?

A) Anything that has the potential to cause harm or damage

B) The level of risk on site

C) A type of barrier or machine guard

D) The likelihood that something might happen

1.13

Why is it important to identify hazards?

A) They have the potential to cause harm

B) They must all be eliminated before work can start

C) They must all be notified to the Health and Safety Executive (HSE)

D) They have to be written on the Health and Safety Law poster

1.14

Who should undertake a planned task that involves significant risk?

A) A competent person

B) A worker

C) A supervisor

D) A health and safety professional

1.15

Two contract workers arrive on site with a file of generic risk assessments. You are keen for them to start but you know the risk assessments do not take into account the current site specific hazards. What is the **best** thing to do?

A) Turn them away and tell them to come back with better paperwork

B) Get them to sign the generic risk assessments and tell them about the site

C) Amend the risk assessments with them or their supervisor, to take into account site specific hazards

D) Cover the site specific hazards during the site induction

Answers: 1.10 = B   1.11 = D   1.12 = A   1.13 = A   1.14 = A   1.15 = C

1.16

Why may a young person be more at risk of having accidents?

- [A] Legislation does not apply to anyone under 18 years of age
- [B] They are usually left to work alone to gain experience
- [C] They have less experience and may not recognise danger or understand what could go wrong
- [D] There is no legal duty to provide them with personal protective equipment (PPE)

1.17

What should be your **first** action if you discover children playing on site?

- [A] Tell the site manager
- [B] Shout and warn them off
- [C] Make sure they are taken to a safe place
- [D] Find out how they got into the site

1.18

The standards of health and safety on a project site have noticeably declined. What is the **first** thing you should do to find out about the contractor's attitude to health and safety?

- [A] Talk to some of the local residents
- [B] Check their RIDDOR reports
- [C] Talk to the site manager
- [D] Call the contractor's safety department

1.19

Why is it important to review and update the site induction regularly?

- [A] It will affect your performance-related pay
- [B] Hazards are likely to change on site as work progresses
- [C] It is a legal requirement to update site inductions on a weekly basis
- [D] It will help to keep the site clean and tidy

1.20

Which of the following has the highest priority under any hierarchy of control?

- [A] Specifying the use of a mobile elevating work platform (MEWP) for steel erection
- [B] Pre-fabrication of steelwork that eliminates the need for a high-level bolted connection
- [C] The installation of a 2 m high barrier to prevent unauthorised access to an area where work at height is taking place
- [D] The introduction of a comprehensive briefing sheet to warn workers of the dangers of working at height

A
01

Answers: 1.16 = C   1.17 = C   1.18 = C   1.19 = B   1.20 = B

A 01

1.21

ERIC is a summary of the general principles of prevention when developing safe methods of work. What does it stand for?

- A Employ, reduce, isolate, control
- B Ensure, reduce, isolate, control
- C Eliminate, reduce, isolate, control
- D Educate, reduce, isolate, control

1.22

From a safety point of view, which of the following should be considered **first** when deciding on the number and location of access and egress points to a site?

- A Off road parking for cars and vans
- B Access for the emergency services
- C Access for heavy vehicles
- D Site security

1.23

Which of the following can provide a good first impression of how well a site is being run?

- A How tidy and organised it is
- B What the principal contractor says in the monthly site meeting
- C What the last RIDDOR report says
- D The number of signs displayed at the site entrance

1.24

Which of the following is **not** a good reason for obtaining and communicating information on construction health risks?

- A Many professionals and workers do not know enough about construction health risks
- B Construction workers do not always understand the long-term effects on their health
- C Ill health in construction workers is more common than traumatic injuries
- D It tests the literacy skills of construction workers

1.25

What is the **best** way for a responsible person to make sure that all who are doing a job have fully understood a method statement?

- A Attach the method statement to the risk assessment and job sheet
- B Explain the method statement to those doing the job and test their understanding
- C Make sure that those doing the job have read the method statement
- D Display the method statements on a noticeboard in the office

1.26

How would you expect the topics for toolbox talks to be selected?

A They should be on safety topics that are in the news

B The topic relates to work that is being carried out at that time

C The client selects the topic for each talk

D In an order so that each topic is given at least once a year

1.27

What is the purpose of using a permit-to-work system?

A To ensure that the job is being carried out properly

B To ensure that the job is carried out by the easiest method

C To enable tools and equipment to be properly checked before work starts

D To control work to prevent a major accident

1.28

Where should you find out the number of people who may be carried in a passenger hoist on site?

A Displayed on a legible notice within the site welfare area

B Displayed on a legible notice within the cage of the hoist

C Given in the company safety policy

D On the health and safety poster

1.29

Welding is about to start on the site you are visiting. What should be provided to prevent passers-by from getting arc eye?

A Warning signs

B Screens

C Personal protective equipment (PPE)

D Pedestrian walkways

1.30

On visiting a site you notice that it is next to a primary school. What is likely to be the most effective way of keeping children off construction sites?

A Putting up 'keep out' posters

B Erecting security fencing or hoarding and keeping all entrance gates closed

C Giving safety talks to the local schools and youth clubs

D Sending a flyer to local households telling them to keep their children off site

A
01

02 Accident reporting and recording

A
02

2.01

Which of these does **not** have to be recorded in the accident book?

- A The injured person's national insurance number
- B The date and time of the accident
- C Details of the injury
- D The home address of the injured person

2.02

When **must** you record an accident in the accident book?

- A If you are injured in any way
- B Only if you have to be off work
- C Only if you have suffered a broken bone
- D Only if you have to go to hospital

2.03

If someone is injured at work, who should record it in the accident book?

- A The site manager
- B The injured person or someone acting for them
- C The first aider
- D Someone from the Health and Safety Executive (HSE)

2.04

Which of the following statements about recording accidents is **true**?

- A They must include details of the next of kin
- B They must only be completed by a site manager or supervisor
- C They must comply with the requirements of the Data Protection Act
- D They must only be kept in an electronic format

2.05

What is the **most** important reason for keeping a working area on a construction site clean and tidy?

- A To prevent slips, trips and falls
- B So that the workers don't have to have a big clean-up at the end of the week
- C So that waste skips can be emptied more often
- D To recycle waste and help the environment

2.06

Why is it important for all workers to attend site induction?

- A Workers will get to know other new starters
- B Risk assessments will be handed out
- C Site-specific health and safety rules will be explained
- D Permits to work will be handed out

Answers: 2.01 = A   2.02 = A   2.03 = B   2.04 = C   2.05 = A   2.06 = C

2.07

Which of the following is the **least** important reason for recording all accidents?

- A It might stop them happening again
- B Some types of accident have to be reported to the Health and Safety Executive (HSE)
- C Details have to be entered in the accident book
- D To find out who is to blame and make sure they are prosecuted

2.08

How can you help to prevent accidents?

- A By acting on reports of unsafe working conditions
- B By becoming a first aider
- C By knowing where the first-aid kit is kept
- D By knowing how to get help quickly

2.09

When are people, who are working on or visiting construction sites, **most likely** to have an accident?

- A In the morning
- B In the afternoon
- C During the summer months
- D When they first start on any new site

2.10

Historically, which type of accident kills the **most** construction workers?

- A Falling from height
- B Contact with electricity
- C Being run over by site transport
- D Being hit by a falling object

A
02

2.11

A scaffold has collapsed and you saw it happen. What should you say when you are asked about the accident?

- A Nothing, as you are not a scaffold expert
- B As little as possible because you don't want to get people into trouble
- C Exactly what you saw
- D Who you think is to blame and how they should be punished

2.12

What is a near miss?

- A An incident where you were just too late to see what happened
- B An incident where someone could have been injured or something could have been damaged
- C An incident where someone was injured and nearly had to go to hospital
- D An incident where someone was injured and nearly had to take time off work

Answers: 2.07 = D   2.08 = A   2.09 = D   2.10 = A   2.11 = C   2.12 = B

2

A
02

2.13

Why is it important to report near miss incidents on site?

- A) Because it is the law to report all near miss incidents
- B) To find someone to blame
- C) It is a requirement of the CDM Regulations
- D) To learn from them and stop them happening again

2.14

A member of the public has been injured by work activities and taken to hospital for treatment. What should happen next?

- A) The accident should be reported by the responsible person to the Health and Safety Executive (HSE)
- B) The responsible person should send the member of the public some flowers and ask them to keep quiet
- C) The member of the public should be reminded by the responsible person to take greater care and attention near a site
- D) The accident should only be reported to the site health and safety manager by the responsible person

2.15

Who **must** be legally notified of a death, specified injury, dangerous occurrence or over seven-day injury on a site?

- A) The company's insurance company
- B) The local health centre
- C) The Health and Safety Executive (HSE)
- D) No-one

2.16

An excavator on site has overturned but no-one was injured. What **must** happen next?

- A) Clear up as quickly as possible and resume work
- B) Investigate the incident
- C) Make a report to the Health and Safety Executive (HSE)
- D) Report the incident in the accident book

2.17

If you have a minor accident, who is responsible for making sure it is reported?

- A) Anyone who saw the accident happen
- B) A workmate
- C) You
- D) The Health and Safety Executive (HSE)

Answers: 2.13 = D   2.14 = A   2.15 = C   2.16 = B   2.17 = C

2.18

When leaving a site you have been visiting you notice that a contractor is working in an unsafe manner. What should you do?

- [A] It is not your responsibility so leave site
- [B] Return and speak to the site manager
- [C] Contact the principal designer
- [D] Contact the contractor's head office

2.19

If your doctor says that you contracted Weil's disease (leptospirosis) on site, why do you need to tell your employer?

- [A] Your employer has to warn your colleagues not to go near you
- [B] Your employer will have to report it to the Health and Safety Executive (HSE)
- [C] Your employer will need to call pest control to remove rats on site
- [D] The site on which you contracted it will have to be closed down

2.20

While on site you see a contractor working in a way that presents an imminent danger to yourself and others around you. What should you do immediately?

A
02

- [A] Move to another area of the site and continue with your work
- [B] Before you leave site ensure that you inform the project manager
- [C] Speak directly to the contractor and tell them to stop
- [D] Ensure that you inform the client and the principal designer

A
02

B

Health and welfare

Contents

03 Health and welfare

3.01

A doctor gives an employee some medication. What question is it important that the employee asks the doctor?

- [A] Will it make them drowsy or unsafe to work or operate machinery?
- [B] Will it make them work more slowly?
- [C] Will they fail a drugs test?
- [D] Will it cause them to oversleep and be late for work?

3.02

You can catch an infection called tetanus from contaminated land or water. How does it get into your body?

- [A] Through your nose when you breathe
- [B] Through an open cut in your skin
- [C] Through your mouth when you eat or drink
- [D] It doesn't, it only infects animals and not people

3.03

Which of the following is most likely to result in those who work with sheet lead having raised levels of lead in their blood?

- [A] By them not using the correct respirator
- [B] By not washing their hands before eating
- [C] By not changing out of their work clothes
- [D] By them not wearing safety goggles

3.04

You suspect someone has been drinking alcohol or is still over the alcohol limit. What should you do?

- [A] Get them to drink plenty of strong coffee before they go back to work
- [B] Tell them your concerns and see that they are safely removed from site
- [C] Ask them to stay away an hour and then go back to work
- [D] Get them to eat and drink something, wait 30 minutes and then go back to work

3.05

Why shouldn't white spirit or other solvents be used to clean hands?

A They could strip the protective oils from the skin

B They could remove the top layer of skin

C They could block the pores of the skin

D They could carry harmful bacteria that attack the skin

3.06

What condition can be caused by direct sunlight exposure on bare skin?

A Dermatitis

B Rickets

C Acne

D Skin cancer

3.07

What can cause occupational dermatitis?

A Hand-arm vibration

B Another person with dermatitis

C Some types of strong chemical

D Sunlight

3.08

What is the **main** issue with using barrier cream to protect the skin?

A There may be none available on site

B Many harmful substances go straight through it

C It is difficult to wash off

D It can irritate your skin

3.09

When site workers need to handle harmful substances, which condition can be prevented by wearing the correct protection gloves?

A Skin disease

B Vibration white finger

C Raynaud's syndrome

D Arthritis

3.10

In what situation is a worker **most** likely to catch Weil's disease (leptospirosis)?

A If they work near wet ground, waterways or sewers

B If they work near air-conditioning units

C If they work fixing showers or baths

D If they drink water from a standpipe

B
03

3.11

What other illness can be easily confused with the early signs of Weil's disease (leptospirosis)?

A Dermatitis

B Diabetes

C Hay fever

D Influenza (flu)

**B
03**

3.12

Which of the following species of animal is the most likely carrier of Weil's disease (leptospirosis) on construction sites?

A Rabbits

B Rats

C Squirrels

D Mice

3.13

The legionella bacteria that cause Legionnaires' disease are most likely to be found in which of the following?

A A boiler operating at a temperature of 80°C

B An infrequently used shower hose outlet

C A cold water storage cistern containing water at 10°C

D A WC toilet pan

3.14

How are legionella bacteria passed on to humans?

A Through fine water droplets, such as sprays or mists

B By drinking dirty water

C Through contact with the skin

D From other people when they sneeze

3.15

What are the legal minimum facilities that should be provided on site for washing your hands?

A Nothing, there is no need to provide washing facilities

B Running hot water and electric hand-dryers

C A cold water standpipe and paper towels

D Hot and cold water (or warm water), soap, and a way to dry hands

3.16

What sort of rest area should be provided for workers on site?

A A covered area

B A covered area and some chairs

C A covered area, tables and chairs with backs, and something to boil water and heat food

D Nothing, contractors don't have to provide rest areas

3.17

What should you do if you find that the toilets on the site you are visiting are dirty?

- A Ignore the problem, it is normal
- B Tell the site manager who can sort it out
- C Ask someone to find some cleaning materials and attend to it
- D See if you can use the toilets in a nearby café or pub

3.18

The site is due to close in one week and the toilets do **not** flush. What should you do?

- A Put a sign on the door explaining that the toilets are out of order
- B Arrange to get the toilets fixed straight away
- C Ask everyone to bear with you as the site is nearly finished
- D Tell the site workers to use the fast food outlet facilities nearby

3.19

When can male and female workers use the same toilet facilities on a construction site?

- A Not in any circumstances
- B If the toilet cubicle is partitioned from any urinals
- C If the toilet is in a lockable room, for use by one person at a time
- D If sanitary waste disposal is provided

3.20

When providing showers for male and female workers, which is the preferred option?

- A Men and women can use the same facilities
- B Provision of cubicles separated by a partition, and recommended for use by one person at a time
- C Provision of facilities in a separate room
- D If they are in a separate cubicle

B
03

04 First aid and emergency procedures

4.01

How do you find out about emergency assembly points?

A By reading a risk assessment

B By reading a method statement

C At the site induction

D By checking the permit to work

4.02

How do workers find out what to do if they are injured on site?

A By asking someone on site

B By looking for the first-aid sign

C By attending a first-aid course

D It should be included at site induction

4.03

How are site-based staff and visitors informed of the location of first-aid facilities on site?

A By walking the site looking for the first-aid sign

B By searching the site office

C By attending the site induction

D By reading the Health and Safety Law poster

4.04

How should site visitors be informed of what to do in the event of an on-site emergency?

A They should study the plans on the wall of the site office

B They are informed during site induction

C They should ask the site manager

D They should take a look around the site for the emergency assembly point

4.05

How can you see for yourself that attention has been given to simple emergency procedures on site?

A Scaffolding has inspection labels fitted

B The distance between the structure and the assembly point is minimised

C There are fire points with extinguishers and a means of raising the alarm

D All electrical appliances have been electrically tested

4.06

Do those in charge of sites have to provide a first-aid box?

A Yes, every site must have one

B Only if more than five people work on site

C Only if more than 25 people work on site

D No, there is no legal duty to provide one

Answers: 4.01 = C   4.02 = D   4.03 = C   4.04 = B   4.05 = C   4.06 = A

4.07

How should workers be informed about what to do in an emergency? Give **two** answers.

- [A] By attending the site induction
- [B] By looking in the health and safety file
- [C] By asking the Health and Safety Executive (HSE)
- [D] By asking at the local hospital
- [E] By reading the site noticeboards

4.08

If there is an emergency while you are on site, what should you do **first**?

- [A] Leave the site and go back to your office
- [B] Phone your office
- [C] Follow the site emergency procedure
- [D] Phone the police

4.09

Where **must** an emergency route or routes ensure safe access to?

- [A] The ground
- [B] The open air
- [C] A place of safety
- [D] The first-aid room

4.10

A survey on a remote unoccupied site needs to be carried out. What should the worker be provided with?

- [A] A suitably stocked first-aid kit
- [B] The first-aid box from the office
- [C] The telephone number for the local HSE office
- [D] A book on first aid

B
04

4.11

When would you expect eyewash bottles to be provided?

- [A] Only on demolition sites where asbestos has to be removed
- [B] Only on sites where refurbishment is being carried out
- [C] On all sites where people could get something in their eyes
- [D] On all sites where showers are needed

4.12

What must a travelling first-aid kit **not** contain?

- [A] Bandages
- [B] Plasters
- [C] Safety pins
- [D] Tablets or medicines

B
04

4.13

If you cut your finger and it won't stop bleeding, what should you do?

A Wrap something around it and carry on working

B Tell the site manager about the problem

C Wash it clean then carry on working

D Find a first aider or get other medical help

4.14

Someone has fallen from height and has no feeling in their legs. What should you do?

A Roll them onto their back and keep their legs straight

B Roll them onto their side and bend their legs

C Ensure they stay still and don't move them until medical help arrives

D Raise their legs to see if any feeling comes back

4.15

If someone is in contact with a live cable, what should you do **first**?

A Phone the electricity company

B Dial 999 and ask for an ambulance

C Switch off the power and call for help

D Pull them away from the cable

4.16

What is the **first** thing you should do if you find an injured person?

A Tell the site manager

B Check that you are not in any danger before you check the injured person

C Move the injured person to a safe place

D Ask the injured person what happened

4.17

Someone working in a deep manhole has collapsed. What is the **first** thing you should do?

A Get someone lowered into the manhole on a rope

B Climb into the manhole and give mouth-to-mouth resuscitation

C Run and tell the site manager

D Shout and raise the alarm as a trained rescue team will be needed

4.18

Someone collapses with stomach pain and there is no first aider on site. What should you do **first**?

A Get them to sit down

B Get someone to call the emergency services

C Get them to lie down in the recovery position

D Give them some painkillers

4.19

If you are **not** trained in first aid, and someone is knocked unconscious, what should you do **first**?

- A) Turn them over so they are lying on their back
- B) Send for medical help
- C) Slap their face to wake them up
- D) Give mouth-to-mouth resuscitation

4.20

What is the one thing a first aider cannot do?

- A) Give mouth-to-mouth resuscitation
- B) Stop any bleeding
- C) Give medicines without authorisation
- D) Treat casualties if they are unconscious

4.21

When an employer's first aid needs assessment indicates that a first aider is unnecessary, the minimum requirement is to ensure that there is an appointed person. Which of the following would you expect an appointed person to carry out?

- A) Provide most of the care normally carried out by a first aider
- B) Provide all of the care normally provided by a first aider
- C) Contact the emergency services and direct them to the scene of an accident
- D) Only apply plasters and dressings to minor wounds

4.22

Which **two** of the following factors must be considered when providing first-aid facilities on site?

- A) The cost of first-aid equipment
- B) The hazards, risks and nature of the work carried out
- C) The number of people expected to be on site at any time
- D) The difficulty in finding time to purchase the necessary equipment
- E) The space in the site office to store the necessary equipment

B
04

4.23

If you think someone has broken a leg, what should you do?

- A) Lie them on their side in the recovery position
- B) Use your belt to strap their legs together
- C) Send for the first aider or get other help
- D) Lie them on their back

4.24

If someone gets grit in their eye, what is the **best** thing to do?

- A) Hold the eye open and wipe it with clean tissue paper
- B) Ask them to rub the eye until it starts to water
- C) Tell them to blink a couple of times
- D) Hold the eye open and flush it with sterilised water or eyewash

Answers: 4.19 = B   4.20 = C   4.21 = C   4.22 = B, C   4.23 = C   4.24 = D

B
04

4.25

Someone gets a large splinter in their hand. It is deep under the skin and it hurts. What should be done?

- A Use something sharp to dig it out
- B Make sure they get first aid
- C Tell them to ignore it and let the splinter come out on its own
- D Try to squeeze out the splinter with your thumbs

4.26

Someone has got a nail in their foot. You are not a first aider. Why must you **not** pull the nail out?

- A You will let air and bacteria get into the wound
- B The nail is helping to reduce the bleeding
- C It will prove that the casualty was not wearing safety boots
- D The nail would become a bio-hazard

4.27

What is the **best** thing to do if someone burns their hand?

- A Tell them to put the hand into cold water or under a cold running tap
- B Tell them to carry on working to exercise the hand
- C Tell them to rub barrier cream or Vaseline® into the burn
- D Tell them to wrap a handkerchief around the burn

05 Personal protective equipment

5.01

While on site you observe that there is a risk of materials flying at speed into site workers' eyes. What should they be wearing to protect themselves?

A Impact-resistant goggles or full face shield

B Welding goggles

C Reading glasses or sunglasses

D Light eye protection

5.02

When should eye protection be worn?

A On very bright, sunny days

B If there is a risk of eye injury and if it is the site rules

C When it has been included in the bill of quantities

D Only for work with chemicals

5.03

What type of eye protection do workers need to wear when they are using a cartridge-operated tool or compressed gas tool, for example, a nail gun?

A Light eye protection or safety glasses

B Normal prescription glasses or sunglasses

C Impact-rated goggles

D None – they aren't needed as there is a minimal risk of injury

5.04

When should you wear safety footwear on site?

A Only when working at ground level or outside

B Until the site starts to look finished

C All the time

D When you are working all day on site and not just visiting

B
05

5.05

What features should you be looking for when obtaining safety footwear for a site visit?

A They must be black with a good sole pattern

B They only need a protective toecap and thin mid-sole

C They must have a protective toecap and mid-sole

D They must be smooth-soled to prevent the transfer of contaminated materials

5.06

Do all types of glove protect hands against chemicals?

A Yes, all gloves are made to the same standard

B Only if site workers put barrier cream on their hands as well

C No, different types of glove protect against different types of hazard

D Only if site workers cover their gloves with barrier cream

B
05

5.07

How should you wear your safety helmet to get maximum protection from it?

 [A] Back to front

 [B] Pushed back on your head

 [C] Square on your head

 [D] Pulled forward

5.08

When is the only time that you do **not** need to wear head protection on site?

[A] If you are working on a project that is at the finishing stages

[B] If you are working where there are no hazards above you

[C] When you are in a safe area, like the site office

[D] If you are working in very hot weather

5.09

What should you do if you drop your safety helmet from height onto a hard surface?

[A] Have any cracks repaired then carry on wearing it

[B] Make sure there are no cracks then carry on wearing it

[C] Work without a safety helmet until you can get a new one

[D] Stop work and get a new safety helmet

5.10

When **must** you wear hi-vis (high visibility) clothing?

[A] When the need is identified in the contractor's or your employer's site rules

[B] Only if you are inspecting deep excavations or tunnels

[C] During normal daylight hours only

[D] Only if you are working alongside moving plant

5.11

What should you do if your personal protective equipment (PPE) gets damaged?

[A] Throw it away and work without it

[B] Stop what you are doing until it is replaced

[C] Carry on wearing it but work more quickly

[D] Try to repair it

5.12

You are about to enter an active work area on site. How will you know if you need any extra personal protective equipment (PPE)?

- [A] By looking at the health and safety policy
- [B] You will always need it
- [C] From the risk assessment or method statement
- [D] Others around you will be wearing more than the minimum PPE required

5.13

Who has the legal duty to ensure that workers are provided with any personal protective equipment (PPE) they need, including the means to maintain it?

- [A] The employer
- [B] The workers who need it
- [C] The client for the project
- [D] The person whose design created the need for the use of PPE

5.14

If employees have to work outdoors in bad weather, why should you supply them with waterproof clothing?

- [A] So they need to take fewer breaks
- [B] They need protecting from the weather and are less likely to get muscle strains if they are warm and dry
- [C] They are less likely to catch Weil's disease (leptospirosis) if they are warm and dry
- [D] They prevent slips and trips

B
05

5.15

Look at these statements about personal protective equipment (PPE). Which one is **not** true?

- [A] Workers must pay for any damage or loss
- [B] Workers must store it correctly when they are not using it
- [C] Workers must report any damage or loss to their manager
- [D] Workers must use it as instructed

5.16

When **must** employers supply personal protective equipment (PPE)?

- [A] Twice a year
- [B] If workers pay for it
- [C] If it is in the contract
- [D] If it is needed to provide protection

Answers: 5.12 = C   5.13 = A   5.14 = B   5.15 = A   5.16 = D

**B
05**

5.17

Do workers have to pay for any personal protective equipment (PPE) they need?

A Yes, they must pay for all of it

B Only to replace lost or damaged PPE

C Yes, but they only have to pay half the cost

D No, the employer must pay for it

5.18

What item of personal protective equipment (PPE), from the following list, should be used when oxyacetylene welding?

A Ear defenders

B Clear goggles

C Eye protection with a tinted or filter lens

D Dust mask

5.19

When working in an area where fibreglass roof insulation is being handled, in addition to safety boots and helmet, which of the following items of personal protective equipment (PPE) should be worn?

A Gloves, respiratory protective equipment and eye protection

B Rubber apron, eye protection and ear defenders

C Ear defenders, respiratory protective equipment and knee pads

D Barrier cream, eye protection and respiratory protective equipment

06 Dust and fumes (Respiratory hazards)

6.01

Someone is using a disc cutter to cut concrete blocks. What **three** immediate hazards are likely to affect them?

A Flying fragments

B Dermatitis

C Harmful dust in the air

D High noise levels

E Skin cancer

6.02

Why is it important to be clean shaven if using a half mask respirator?

A The filter material will become blocked more quickly

B You may suffer an allergic reaction to the mask

C Facial hair can affect the seal around your face

D You will be able to use the same mask for longer

6.03

Where are workers likely to breathe in the highest quantities of dust when drilling, cutting, sanding or grinding?

A Outside on a still day

B Outside on a windy day

C In a small room

D In a large indoor space

6.04

What should you **not** encourage workers to do when they are sweeping up?

A Dampen down the area

B Make sure there is plenty of ventilation

C Wear their protective mask

D Dry sweep the area quickly

6.05

What should a worker do if the water they are using to control dust runs out?

A Put on additional respiratory protection

B Stop and refill the water

C Ask everyone to clear the area and then carry on

D Carry on but get someone to sweep up afterwards

6.06

What is the **best** way to limit dust exposure when assessing the use of a power tool?

A Stop dust getting into the air

B Provide adequate ventilation

C Find a way to do the work quickly to limit dust exposure

D Only undertake the work during damp or wet weather

B
06

Answers: 6.01 = A, C, D   6.02 = C   6.03 = C   6.04 = D   6.05 = B   6.06 = A

6.07

Work is being planned that will create dust. What action should be taken?

A The work should not be carried out because dust is highly dangerous

B Equipment to eliminate or reduce dust and personal protective equipment (PPE) suitable for the work should be used

C Work should commence – no controls are needed as dust cannot cause serious harm or injury

D Work for short periods at a time

6.08

What **must** workers ensure when using water to keep dust down when cutting?

A That there is as much water as possible

B That the water flow is correctly adjusted

C That somebody stands next to them to pour water from a bottle

D That water is poured onto the surface before they start cutting

6.09

Work is planned that needs to use a power tool to cut or grind materials. Select the **two** best ways to control the dust.

A Work slowly and carefully

B Fit a dust extractor or collector to the machine

C Wet cutting

D Keep the area clean and tidy

E Wear a dust mask

6.10

When using a power tool to cut or grind materials, why must the dust be collected and **not** allowed to get into the air?

A To save time and avoid having to clear up the mess

B Most dust can be harmful if breathed in

C The tool will be faster if the dust is collected

D A machine guard is not needed if the dust is collected

6.11

What should workers do if they find pigeon droppings and nests in an area where they are required to work?

A Carry on with the work carefully, so they don't disturb them

B Stop work and seek advice

C Try to catch the pigeons

D Wait for the pigeons to fly away before carrying on with the work

6.12

What illness can be caused by breathing in a dusty atmosphere for long periods of time?

A Occupational asthma

B Occupational dermatitis

C Skin cancer

D Weil's disease (leptospirosis)

B
06

Answers: 6.07 = B   6.08 = B   6.09 = B, C   6.10 = B   6.11 = B   6.12 = A

6.13

What can cause occupational asthma?

A Exposure to loud noise

B Exposure to rat urine

C Skin contact with any hazardous substance

D Breathing in hazardous dust, fumes or vapours

6.14

What is the biggest cause of long-term health issues in the construction industry?

A Loud noise

B Being struck by a vehicle

C Slipping and tripping

D Breathing in hazardous dust and fumes

6.15

What should workers do if they have been given a dust mask to protect them against hazardous fumes?

A Only start work when they have the correct respiratory protective equipment (RPE)

B Start work wearing the dust mask but work quickly

C Start work but take regular breaks

D Wear a second dust mask on top of the first one

6.16

Your workers have been face-fit tested. What is **one** of the checks you can make to ensure their mask provides a tight seal?

A That they are clean shaven

B That they have no more than two days' stubble growth

C That they have no more than one week's stubble growth

D That their voices cannot be heard when wearing the mask

6.17

Disposable masks have filtering facepiece ratings of FFP1, FFP2 and FFP3. Which offers the greater protection?

A FFP1

B FFP2

C FFP3

D They all offer the same protection, the numbers refer to the different sizes of mask

6.18

Which of the following do you **not** need to do to ensure that someone's mask works?

A Check the mask is the correct type needed

B Check the wearer has passed a face-fit test wearing the mask

C Check it is being worn correctly

D Immerse it in water to ensure the seals are tight

B
06

6.19

How long can you use the same disposable half mask respirator for? Select **two** answers.

A Until it is visibly contaminated

B A single shift (8 hours)

C 5 working days

D 14 days

E 28 days

6.20

Which of these activities does **not** create harmful silica dust?

A Sawing timber and plywood

B Cutting kerbs, stone, paving slabs, bricks and blocks

C Breaking up concrete floors and screeds

D Chasing out walls and mortar joints or sweeping up rubble

6.21

Which of the following is **not** a health effect of being exposed to paints and resins which have high levels of solvents?

A Headaches and sickness

B Drowsiness or poor co-ordination

C Dermatitis or skin problems

D Hearing loss

6.22

When drilling, cutting, sanding or grinding what is the **best** way to protect your long-term health from harmful dust?

A Use dust extraction or wet cut and wear a hard hat, hi-vis jacket and light eye protection

B Wear FFP3-rated respiratory protective equipment (RPE) and impact goggles

C Wear any disposable dust mask, a hard hat, hi-vis jacket, hearing protection and impact goggles

D Use dust extraction or wet cut, wear FFP3-rated respiratory protective equipment (RPE), hearing protection and impact goggles

07 Noise and vibration

7.01

Can the damage by exposure to noise over a long period of time be reversed?

A Yes, with time

B Yes, if you have an operation

C No, the damage is permanent

D Yes, if you change jobs

7.02

How can noise affect someone's health? Give **two** answers.

A Headaches

B Ear infections

C Permanent hearing loss

D Waxy ears

E Dizziness and nausea

7.03

What does it mean if someone has a ringing sound in their ears after working with noisy equipment?

A Their hearing has been temporarily damaged

B They have also been subjected to vibration

C Their hearing protection was working properly

D The noise level was high but acceptable

7.04

Noise can cause damage to people's hearing. What is an early sign of this?

A There are no early signs

B Temporary deafness or a ringing noise in the ears

C A skin rash around the ears

D Regular ear infections

7.05

When referring to noise, what does the term **upper exposure action value** mean?

A The level at which hearing protection zones must be established and hearing protection must be worn

B The second time a noise reading is taken during a controlled measurement of site noise

C The loudest a noise can be before work with the tools causing the noise must stop

D The highest noise reading from a representative sample

7.06

What does wearing hearing protection do?

A Stops you hearing all noise

B Reduces damaging noise to an acceptable level

C Repairs your hearing if it is damaged

D Makes you hear better

B
07

7.07

What **must** you remember if you need to wear hearing protection?

A You have to carry out your own noise assessment

B You have to pay for all hearing protection

C Earplugs don't work

D You may be less aware of what is going on around you

7.08

What are **two** recommended ways to protect your hearing?

A Rolled tissue paper

B Cotton wool pads over your ears

C Earplugs

D Soft cloth pads over your ears

E Ear defenders

7.09

What should you do if a worker needs to wear ear defenders but an ear pad is missing from one of the shells?

A Tell them not to wear them, and to work without hearing protection

B Tell them to put them on and go to site with them as they are

C Tell them they cannot work in any noisy area until the ear defenders are replaced

D Tell them to take an ear pad from another set of ear defenders

7.10

Someone near you is using noisy equipment and you have no hearing protection. What should you do?

A Ask them to stop what they are doing

B Carry on with your work as you are not the person using the equipment

C Leave the area until you have the correct personal protective equipment (PPE)

D Speak to the operative's supervisor

7.11

You have to inspect a site near a construction operation that is generating a high level of noise. It is **not** possible to shut the operation down. Which of the following actions would you expect to be the site manager's immediate response?

A Arrange for a noise assessment to be carried out

B Make hearing protection available to those people who ask for it

C Issue all people affected with hearing protection as a precaution

D Erect hearing protection zone signs

Answers: 7.07 = D   7.08 = C, E   7.09 = C   7.10 = C   7.11 = C

7.12

What **must** you do if you have to enter a hearing protection zone?

A Not make any noise

B Wear the correct hearing protection at all times

C Take hearing protection with you in case you need to use it

D Wear hearing protection if the noise gets too loud for you

7.13

Noise levels may be a general problem if you have to shout to be understood when someone is standing how far away?

A 2 m away

B 4 m away

C 5 m away

D 6 m away

7.14

What is the significance of the weekly or daily personal noise exposure limit value of 87 decibel (dBA) set out in the Control of Noise at Work Regulations?

A All site personnel and visitors need to be warned if this noise level is being exceeded

B Hearing protection needs to be provided upon request if this level is likely to be exceeded

C The principal contractor must make sure everyone carries their hearing protection if this noise level is exceeded

D Employers must ensure that their personnel are not exposed to noise above this level

B
07

7.15

If you need to wear disposable foam earplugs how should you insert them so they protect your hearing from damage?

A Soak them in water, squeeze them out and then insert them into your ear canal

B Do not roll or fold them, and insert them half way into your ear canal

C Roll them up and insert them as far as you can, while pulling the top of your ear up to open up the ear canal

D Fold them in half, pull on your earlobe and wedge them into your ear

7.16

Why is over exposure to vibratory tools and equipment a serious issue?

A There are no early warning signs

B The long-term effects of vibration are not known

C There is no way that exposure to vibration can be prevented

D Vibration can cause a disabling injury that cannot be cured

7.17

What is vibration white finger?

A A mild skin rash that will go away

B A serious skin condition that will not clear up

C Industrial dermatitis

D A sign of damage to someone's hands that might not go away

7.18

What health problem can be caused by hand-arm vibration syndrome (HAVS)?

A Skin cancer

B Skin irritation, like dermatitis

C Blisters on hands and arms

D Damaged blood vessels and nerves in fingers and hands

7.19

Who should you inform if someone reports to you that they have work-related hand-arm vibration syndrome?

A The Health and Safety Executive (HSE)

B The local Health Authority

C The tool manufacturer

D The nearest hospital

7.20

Which of these tools is **most** likely to cause vibration white finger?

A Handsaw

B Hammer drill

C Hammer and chisel

D Battery-powered screwdriver

7.21

Operatives using machinery that can cause vibration are less likely to suffer from hand-arm vibration syndrome if they feel which of the following?

A Very cold but dry

B Cold and wet

C Warm and dry

D Very wet but warm

Answers: 7.16 = D   7.17 = D   7.18 = D   7.19 = A   7.20 = B   7.21 = C

7.22

What is the **least** reliable source of information when assessing the level of vibration from a powered percussive hand tool?

A In-use vibration measurement of the tool

B Vibration figures taken from the tool manufacturer's handbook

C The judgement of the site manager based upon observation

D Vibration data from the Health and Safety Executive's (HSE) master list

B
07

08 Hazardous substances

8.01

Which one of these is **not** a primary purpose of an asbestos survey?

- A) To provide accurate information on the location, amount and condition of asbestos materials
- B) To identify all asbestos materials that need to be removed before demolition or refurbishment work
- C) To assist in the management of any asbestos in a building
- D) To estimate how much it would cost to remove any asbestos

8.02

What illness might a worker develop if they breathe in asbestos dust?

- A) Aching muscles and painful joints
- B) Throat infections
- C) Lung diseases
- D) Dizziness and headaches

8.03

When visiting site the contractor thinks that they have found some asbestos. What is the **first** thing that should be done?

- A) Stop work and get everyone out of the affected area
- B) Take a sample to the site manager
- C) Put it in the bin and carry on working
- D) Find the first aider

8.04

Which of these statements does **not** apply to asbestos?

- A) It is a dust
- B) It is fibrous
- C) It is likely to be found in buildings built or refurbished before 2000
- D) It is not harmful to health

8.05

You are visiting a site where an active asbestos removal enclosure has been set up. Which of the following would indicate that it is operating efficiently?

- A) There is appropriate signage
- B) Everyone is wearing red suits
- C) The sides of the enclosure are bowing in
- D) Everyone is wearing respiratory protective equipment (RPE)

8.06

Which of these is the **least** likely to cause skin problems?

- A) Asbestos
- B) Bitumens
- C) Epoxy resins
- D) Solvents

Answers: 8.01 = D   8.02 = C   8.03 = A   8.04 = D   8.05 = C   8.06 = A

8.07

If asbestos is present what should happen before demolition or refurbishment takes place?

A Advise workers that asbestos is present and continue with demolition

B All asbestos should be removed as far as reasonably practicable

C The Health and Safety Executive (HSE) should be advised that asbestos is present and the demolition continued

D Inspect the condition of the asbestos materials

8.08

What kind of survey is required to identify asbestos prior to any **invasive** work being carried out on a pre-2000 building?

A Type 3 survey

B Management survey

C Refurbishment or demolition survey

D Type 2 survey

8.09

Where are you **most** likely to come across asbestos?

A In a house built between 1950 and 2005

B In any building built or refurbished before the year 2000

C In industrial buildings built after the year 2000

D Asbestos has now been removed from all buildings

8.10

Following the removal of asbestos when should a certificate of reoccupation be issued?

A After the completion of licensed asbestos work

B After the completion of notifiable non-licensed work

C After the completion of non-licensed asbestos work

D Always, following the removal of any asbestos

8.11

What is the preferred method of checking for leaks when assembling liquefied petroleum gas equipment before use?

A Test with a lighted match

B Sniff the connections to detect the smell of gas

C Listen to hear for escaping gas

D Apply leak detection fluid to the connections

8.12

Why should workers **not** kneel in wet cement, screed or concrete?

A It will make their trousers wet

B It is not an effective way to work

C It can cause serious chemical burns to their legs

D It will affect the finish

B
08

Answers: 8.07 = B   8.08 = C   8.09 = B   8.10 = A   8.11 = D   8.12 = C

B
08

8.13

Why are wet cement, mortar and concrete hazardous to your health?

- A They can cause dizziness and headaches
- B They can cause skin burns and dermatitis
- C They can cause muscle aches
- D They can cause arc eye

8.14

You have to use a new substance for the first time and need to carry out a COSHH assessment. What are the **two** main things you will need?

- A The company's safety policy
- B The safety data sheet
- C The age of the people doing the work
- D The material delivery note
- E Details of where, who and how the substance will be used

8.15

What is the safest way to use a hazardous substance?

- A Getting on with the job as quickly as possible
- B Reading the employer's health and safety policy
- C Understanding the COSHH assessment and following the instructions
- D Asking someone who has already used it

8.16

When a contractor is assessing the risk of using a substance they believe to be hazardous, what should they do **first**?

- A Review the safety data sheet
- B Ensure that safe storage is available on site
- C Ensure workers are provided with respiratory equipment
- D Ensure workers are trained to use respiratory equipment

8.17

What do the COSHH Regulations deal with?

- A The safe use of tools and equipment
- B The safe use of lifting equipment
- C The control and safe use of substances hazardous to health
- D Safe working at height

8.18

Which of the following provides health and safety information about a hazardous substance?

- A The site diary
- B The delivery note
- C The COSHH assessment
- D The manual handling assessment

Answers: 8.13 = B   8.14 = B, E   8.15 = C   8.16 = A   8.17 = C   8.18 = C

8.19

An assessment has been carried out under the COSHH Regulations. Who should the risks and control measures be explained to?

A Everyone working on site

B Those on site who are using, or likely to be affected by, the substance

C The person in charge of ordering materials

D The accounts department

8.20

If it is not reasonably practicable to prevent exposure of workers to substances hazardous to health, which of the following should you consider **first**?

A What instruction, training and supervision to provide

B What health surveillance arrangements will be needed

C How to minimise risk and control exposure

D How to monitor the exposure of workers in the workplace

8.21

How should cylinders containing liquefied petroleum gas (LPG) be stored on site?

A In a locked cellar with clear warning signs

B In a locked cage at least 3 m from any oxygen cylinders

C Within a secure storage container at the back of the site

D Covered by a tarpaulin to shield the compressed cylinder from sunlight

B
08

8.22

Apart from the cylinders used in gas-powered forklift trucks, why should you never see liquefied petroleum gas (LPG) cylinders placed on their side during use?

A It would give a faulty reading on the contents gauge, resulting in flashback

B Air could be drawn into the cylinder, creating a dangerous mixture of gases

C The liquid gas would be at too low a level to allow the torch to burn correctly

D The liquid gas could be drawn from the cylinder, creating a safety hazard

8.23

Which of the following is the safest place to store oxyacetylene gas welding bottles when they are not in use?

A) Outside in a special secure storage compound

B) In company vehicles

C) Inside the building in a locked cupboard

D) In the immediate work area, ready for use the next day

8.24

Where should liquefied petroleum gas (LPG) cylinders be positioned when supplying an appliance in a site cabin?

A) Inside the cabin in a locked cupboard

B) Under the cabin

C) Inside the cabin next to the appliance

D) Outside the cabin

8.25

When observing the use of oxyacetylene-welding equipment, how should the bottles be positioned?

A) Laid on their side

B) Stood upright

C) Stood upside down

D) Angled at 45°

8.26

Which of the following makes it essential for contractors to take great care when handling oxygen cylinders?

A) They contain highly flammable compressed gas

B) They contain highly flammable liquid gas

C) They are filled to extremely high pressures

D) They contain poisonous gas

8.27

You are visiting a project that involves removing paint from old iron work. Which of the following would enable the contractor to assess the foreseeable health risk of the work during the tender period?

A) Laboratory test results of a sample of paint that gives its lead content

B) The prevailing wind conditions

C) Fit testing of respiratory protective equipment (RPE)

D) Tests to determine the average paint thickness

B
08

Answers: 8.23 = A   8.24 = D   8.25 = B   8.26 = C   8.27 = A

8.28

 If you see this label on a substance what should you do?

A Do not use it as the substance is poisonous

B Find out what protection you need as the substance is corrosive and can damage your skin upon contact

C Wash your hands after you have used the substance

D Find out what hand cleaner you will need as the substance will not wash off easily

8.29

 If you see this label on a substance what should you do?

A Find out what protection you need as the substance is harmful and could damage your health

B Use sparingly, as the substance is expensive

C Wear gloves, as the substance can burn your skin

D Do not use it, as the substance is poisonous

8.30

 If you see this label on a substance what should you do?

A Make sure it is stored out of the reach of children

B Make sure it is used carefully and that workers are not spilled or splashed on

C Make sure the substance is not used, as it is poisonous

D Find out what protection is needed as the substance is toxic, even in low quantities

B
08

8.31

How can you tell if a product is hazardous?

A By warning symbols on the container or packaging label

B By the shape of the container

C It will always be in a black container

D It will always be in a cardboard box

8.32

 If you see this label on a substance what should you do?

A Find out how to handle the substance as it is fragile

B Find out how to use the substance safely as it could explode

C Find out how to use the substance safely as it is flammable (could catch fire easily)

D Do not use the substance as it could kill you

Answers: 8.28 = B   8.29 = A   8.30 = D   8.31 = A   8.32 = B

B
08

8.33

 If you see this label on a substance what should you do?

- A Dispose of the substance or contents by burning
- B Find out how to use the substance safely as it could explode
- C Find out how to use the substance safely as it is flammable (could catch fire easily)
- D Warm up the contents first, with heat or a naked flame

8.34

What is the colour of an acetylene cylinder?

- A Orange
- B Black
- C Green
- D Maroon

8.35

You are visiting a site where flooring is being stuck down by a lone worker, using a liquid adhesive in a small inner room that has no visible means of ventilation. What should you quickly bring to the attention of the worker and the supervisor?

- A It is illegal for anyone to work on their own
- B The work should be carried out under a hot-work permit
- C Kneeling and working is bad for their back
- D The vapours from the adhesive may be a health hazard without sufficient fresh air

8.36

You find an unmarked container that you think might contain chemicals. What is the **first** thing you should do?

- A Smell the chemical to see what it is
- B Put it in a bin to get rid of it
- C Move it to somewhere safe
- D Ensure that it remains undisturbed and report it

09 Manual handling

9.01

What **must** all workers do under the regulations for manual handling?

- A Only exceed the weights identified in the risk assessment if they know they are capable of lifting them
- B Make a list of all the heavy things they have to carry
- C Lift any size of load they feel comfortable with
- D Follow the requirements of their employer's safe systems of work

9.02

If manual lifting activities are part of a task, what **must** be carried out?

- A The lifting operations must be supervised
- B A risk assessment of the task must be carried out
- C Nothing, as it is part of some work operations to lift loads
- D Make sure someone watches while the load is lifted

9.03

You are in charge of a gang of workers who are about to start on a new site. What can you do to help minimise manual handling?

- A Remind them not to do any manual handling
- B Hire in extra labour to carry the materials and equipment
- C Assess and agree with the site manager how the materials and equipment can be distributed close to the workplace
- D Make sure the risk assessment has included your workers

B
09

9.04

Your workforce are lifting loads heavier than those recommended in the risk assessment. What should you do?

- A Find out how much they are lifting and change the risk assessment to this weight
- B Warn them but let them carry on
- C Let them carry on as no injuries have occurred
- D Stop them, find out why, agree a solution and amend the risk assessment

Answers: 9.01 = D   9.02 = B   9.03 = C   9.04 = D

B
09

9.05

Who should be involved in creating the manual handling safe system of work for a worker?

A) The worker

B) The worker's supervisor or employer

C) The worker and their supervisor or employer

D) The Health and Safety Executive (HSE)

9.06

A worker is using a wheelbarrow to move a heavy load. Is this manual handling?

A) No, because the wheelbarrow is carrying the load

B) Only if the load slips off the wheelbarrow

C) Yes, they are still manually handling the load

D) Only if the wheelbarrow is pulled instead of pushed

9.07

A worker needs to carry out a task that involves manual handling of survey equipment in and out of vehicles. An old injury means that the worker has a weak back. What should you do?

A) Tell them to take care

B) Review the risk assessment and consider other means of carrying out the task

C) Tell them to try some lifting and then report back

D) Tell them they'll have to find someone else to do the work if they cannot complete it

9.08

A worker has been asked to move a load that might be too heavy for them. They cannot divide it into smaller parts and there is no-one to help them. What should you do?

A) Make sure that they do not move the load until a safe method is identified

B) Ask another worker to get a forklift truck

C) Tell them to try to lift it using the correct lifting methods

D) Tell them to lift and move the load quickly to avoid injuring themselves

9.09

How should a worker stand if they need to lift a load from the floor?

A) Feet together, legs straight and back bent

B) Feet together and knees bent, in a deep squatting position

C) Feet slightly apart, one leg slightly forward and knees flexed

D) Feet wide apart, legs straight and back bent

9.10

What does it mean if lifting and placing a particular load forces a worker to have to twist or turn their body?

A) That the weight they can lift safely is less than usual

B) That the weight they can lift safely is more than usual

C) That they can lift the same weight as usual

D) That they must wear a back brace

9.11

Someone has to move a load while they are sitting down. How much can they move safely?

A) Less than usual

B) The usual amount

C) Twice the usual amount

D) Three times the usual amount

9.12

A heavy load has been delivered to site. What is the **first** thing that should be considered?

A) How far the load would have to be carried manually

B) How the risk of manual handling could be reduced

C) How many people are needed to lift the load

D) How the need to manually lift the load could be avoided

9.13

Manual handling assessment involves four main areas. What are they?

A) Testing, load, environment, individual

B) Environment, individual, task, levels

C) Task, individual, load, environment

D) Individual, energy, task, load

B
09

B
09

C

General safety

Contents

10 Safety signs

10.01

 What are blue and white signs?

A Mandatory signs – meaning you must do something

B Prohibition signs – meaning you must not do something

C Warning signs – alerting you to hazards or danger

D Safe condition signs – giving you information

C 10

10.02

 What does this sign mean?

A Wear hearing protection if you want to

B You must wear hearing protection

C No personal electronic devices

D Caution, noisy machinery

10.03

 What does this sign mean?

A Safety glasses cleaning station

B Warning, bright lights or lasers

C Caution, poor lighting

D You must wear safety eye protection

10.04

 What does this sign mean?

A Safety boots or safety shoes must be worn

B Wellington boots must be worn

C Be aware of slip and trip hazards

D No dirty footwear past this point

10.05

 What does this sign mean?

A You must carry safety gloves at all times

B Dispose of used safety gloves here

C Safety gloves do not need to be worn

D Safety gloves must be worn

10.06

 What does this sign mean?

A Only white safety helmets allowed in this area

B Remove safety helmets in this area

C Safety helmets must be worn

D Dispose of damaged safety helmets here

10.07

 What does this sign mean?

A Safety overalls must be worn

B Only white overalls allowed in this area

C Remove overalls in this area

D Long-sleeved tops must be worn

10.08

 What are round red and white signs with a diagonal line?

A Mandatory signs – meaning you must do something

B Prohibition signs – meaning you must not do something

C Warning signs – alerting you to hazards or danger

D Safe condition signs – giving you information

10.09

 What does this sign mean?

A No lone working

B No entry without a hard hat

C No access for pedestrians

D No entry during the day

10.10

 What does this sign mean?

A Do not use the tap

B Not for washing

C Not drinkable

D Do not wash your vehicle

10.11

 What does this sign mean?

A No gloves

B Do not touch

C Stop button

D Use the handrail

C
10

10.12

 What does this sign mean?

A No mobile phones

B Wifi enabled area

C Mobile phones are allowed

D Mobile phone charging point

Answers: 10.07 = A   10.08 = B   10.09 = C   10.10 = C   10.11 = B   10.12 = A

10.13

 What are green and white signs?

A Mandatory signs – meaning you must do something

B Prohibition signs – meaning you must not do something

C Warning signs – alerting you to hazards or danger

D Safe condition signs – giving you information

10.14

 What does this sign mean?

A Escape route or emergency exit is to the right

B Open the door by sliding it to the right

C One-way pedestrian route

D The site entrance is to the right

10.15

 What does this sign mean?

A Emergency assembly point

B Fire point

C Accident and emergency department

D First aid

10.16

What colour are emergency and safe condition signs, such as fire exit and first aid points?

A Blue and white

B Red and white

C Green and white

D Red and yellow

10.17

 What does this sign mean?

A Toilets and shower facilities

B Drying area for wet weather clothes

C Emergency shower

D Fire sprinklers above

10.18

 What does this sign mean?

A Safety glasses cleaning station

B Emergency eyewash

C Warning, risk of splashing

D Wear eye protection

C 10

Answers: 10.13 = D   10.14 = A   10.15 = D   10.16 = C   10.17 = C   10.18 = B

10.19

 What are yellow and black signs?

A Mandatory signs – meaning you must do something

B Prohibition signs – meaning you must not do something

C Warning signs – alerting you of hazards or danger

D Safe condition signs – giving you information

10.20

 What does this sign mean?

A Dispose of substance or contents by burning

B Warning – substance or contents are combustible or flammable (can catch fire easily)

C Warning – substance or contents could explode

D Warning – substance or contents are harmful

10.21

 What does this sign mean?

A Plant operators wanted

B Industrial vehicles operating

C Manual handling is not allowed

D Storage area

10.22

 What does this sign mean?

A Radioactive material

B Warning – rotating object

C High voltage

D Warning – laser beams

C
10

11 Fire prevention and control

11.01

What is the **first** thing you should do if you discover a fire?

- [A] Put any equipment away
- [B] Finish what you are doing, if it is safe to do so
- [C] Try to put out the fire
- [D] Raise the alarm

11.02

Where should you go if you hear the fire alarm?

- [A] To the site entrance
- [B] To the assembly point
- [C] To the site office
- [D] To the welfare facilities

11.03

What happens to the nozzle of a carbon dioxide (CO_2) fire extinguisher when it is used?

- [A] It gets very cold
- [B] It gets very hot
- [C] It gets very warm
- [D] It gets very heavy

11.04

Which **two** extinguishers should **not** be used on electrical fires?

- [A] Dry powder (blue colour band)
- [B] Foam (cream colour band)
- [C] Water (red colour band)
- [D] Carbon dioxide (black colour band)

11.05

What type of fire extinguisher should **not** be provided where petrol or diesel is being stored?

- [A] Foam
- [B] Water
- [C] Dry powder
- [D] Carbon dioxide

11.06

 A water fire extinguisher, identified by a red band, should **only** be used on what type of fire?

- [A] Wood, paper, textile and solid material fires
- [B] Flammable liquids (fuel, oil, varnish, paints, etc.)
- [C] Electrical fires
- [D] Metal and molten metal

11.07

 A foam extinguisher, identified by a cream band, should **not** be used on what type of fire?

A) Wood, paper and textile fires

B) Flammable liquids
(fuel, oil, varnish, paints, etc.)

C) Solid material fires

D) Electrical fires

11.08

What does it mean if you see frost around the valve on a liquefied petroleum gas (LPG) cylinder?

A) The cylinder is nearly empty

B) The cylinder is full

C) The valve is leaking

D) You must lay the cylinder on its side

11.09

What does a fire need to burn, in addition to heat and fuel?

A) Oxygen

B) Carbon dioxide

C) Argon

D) Nitrogen

11.10

What is HSG168 Fire Safety in Construction?

A) Information given to emergency service crews when attending fires on construction sites

B) A directory of all known construction site fires

C) The Health and Safety Executive's (HSE) guidance for those managing and carrying out construction work

D) The standard for the colour coding of fire extinguishers

11.11

As a result of risk assessment, work is to be carried out under a hot-work permit. What **must** the permit specify?

A) That the work is carried out at a time when the site is otherwise unoccupied

B) That the work is completed immediately before the end of the working day

C) That the work is completed at least one hour before the site closes

D) That the work is completed one hour after the permit expires

C
11

11.12

For safety reasons how should you store or use liquefied petroleum gas (LPG) cylinders used for heating the site cabin?

- A They must be located outside the cabin
- B They must be located inside the cabin but away from the heat source
- C They must be connected to the heat source by flexible rubber tubing
- D They must be lying on their side

11.13

How would you expect highly flammable materials to be stored?

- A In the site storage container
- B Against the hoarding, furthest away from the site offices
- C In a secure compound in the open air
- D Stored in the back of the contractor's vehicle

11.14

How should acetylene and oxygen cylinders that are **not** in use be stored?

- A Together on a bottle trolley
- B Separately and away from site accommodation
- C Lying down so that they cannot fall over and damage the valves
- D Together but away from site accommodation

11.15

What **must** contractors ensure when work is taking place in a corridor that is a fire escape route?

- A That tools, equipment and materials do not block the route
- B That all doors into the corridor are locked
- C That only spark-proof tools are used
- D That all fire escape signs are removed before work starts

11.16

What should be in place on all construction sites to ensure fire precautions are adequately assessed?

- A A fire risk assessment that is updated on an annual basis
- B Hot-work permits
- C A construction phase health and safety plan
- D A fire risk assessment that is regularly updated to reflect current site conditions

11.17

What are **two** common fire risks on construction sites?

- A 230 volt power tools
- B Poor housekeeping and build up of waste
- C Timber racks
- D Uncontrolled hot works
- E 110 volt extension reels

C
11

12 Electrical safety, tools and equipment

12.01

What **two** things can be done to reduce trips and injuries caused by untidy leads and extension cables?

- A Running cables and leads above head height and over the top of doorways and walkways
- B Tying any excess cables and leads up into the smallest coil possible
- C Keeping trailing cables and leads close to the wall
- D Making sure your cables have not been used before
- E Only allowing thinner 230 volt extension cables to be used

12.02

What is the **best** way to protect an extension cable and also reduce trip hazards?

- A Run the cable above head height
- B Run the cable by the shortest route
- C Cover the cable with yellow tape
- D Cover the cable with pieces of wood

12.03

What should you do if a worker tells you that a guard is missing from a power tool?

- A Ask them to try to make another guard
- B Tell them to use the tool, but to work quickly
- C Make sure that they do not use the tool until a proper guard has been fitted
- D Allow them to use the tool, working slowly and carefully

12.04

What guidance should you give a worker who needs to use a power tool with a rotating blade?

- A Remove the guard so that they can clearly see the blade
- B Adjust the guard to expose just enough blade to let them do the job
- C Remove the guard but wear leather gloves to protect their hands
- D Adjust the guard to expose the maximum amount of blade

C
12

C
12

12.05

What are the **two** main functions of the guards on cutting and grinding machines?

- A) To stop materials getting onto the blade or wheel
- B) To give the operator a firm handhold
- C) To balance the machine
- D) To stop fragments flying into the air
- E) To stop the operator coming into contact with the blade or wheel

12.06

Someone near you is using a rotating laser level. What is the health hazard likely to affect you?

- A) Skin cancer
- B) None, if used correctly they are safe
- C) Gradual blindness
- D) Burning of the skin, similar to sunburn

12.07

Why is it dangerous to run an abrasive wheel faster than its recommended maximum speed?

- A) The wheel will get clogged and stop
- B) The motor could burst into flames
- C) The wheel could shatter into many pieces
- D) The safety guard cannot be used

12.08

When is it safe for operatives to work close to an overhead power line?

- A) If they do not touch the line for more than 30 seconds
- B) If they use a wooden ladder
- C) If the power is switched off
- D) If it is not raining

12.09

You are inspecting a site where there are overhead electric cables. What **two** arrangements should a contractor have in place to alert those on site to the presence of the cables?

- A) Scaffolding fan
- B) Warning signs
- C) Gates
- D) Barriers and height restriction goalposts
- E) Traffic lights

12.10

Someone near you is using a disc cutter to cut concrete blocks. What **three** immediate hazards are likely to affect you?

- A) Flying fragments
- B) Dermatitis
- C) Harmful dust in the air
- D) High noise levels
- E) Vibration white finger

Answers: 12.05 = D, E   12.06 = B   12.07 = C   12.08 = C   12.09 = B, D
12.10 = A, C, D

12.11

When should tools and equipment be checked for damage?

A Before each use

B Every day

C Once a week

D At least once a year

12.12

What **two** main areas of visual inspection should be carried out before each use of a power tool?

A Check the carry case isn't broken

B Check the power lead, plug and casing are in good condition

C Check the manufacturer's label hasn't come off

D Check switches, triggers and guards are adjusted and work correctly

E Check it is marked with a security stamp

12.13

Why **must** a RCD (residual current device) be used in conjunction with 230 volt electrical equipment?

A It lowers the voltage

B It quickly cuts off the power if there is a fault

C It makes the tool run at a safe speed

D It saves energy and lowers costs

12.14

How could a site worker check if the RCD (residual current device) through which a 230 volt hand tool is connected to the supply is working correctly?

A Switch the tool on and off

B Press the test button on the RCD unit

C Use a handheld RCD test meter

D Run the tool at top speed to see if it cuts out

12.15

 What does this warning sign mean?

A High voltage

B Risk of radiation

C Electrical appliance

D Risk of lightning

C
12

12.16

What colour should a 110 volt power cable and connector be?

A Black

B Red

C Blue

D Yellow

12.17

Why do building sites use a 110 volt electricity supply instead of a 230 volt domestic supply?

A It is cheaper

B It is less likely to kill people

C It moves faster along the cables

D It is safer for the environment

12.18

What do a yellow plug and a yellow supply cable fitted to an electrical hand tool indicate?

A It shows that the tool runs off a 110 volt supply

B It shows that the tool is waterproof and can be used outdoors in wet conditions

C It shows that the tool runs off a 230 volt supply and should not be used on site

D It shows that the tool has been PAT tested within the past 12 months

12.19

What is the recommended safe voltage for electrical equipment on building sites?

A 12 volts

B 24 volts

C 110 volts

D 230 volts

12.20

In the colour coding of electrical power supplies on site, what voltage does a blue plug represent?

A 50 volts

B 110 volts

C 230 volts

D 400 volts

12.21

On the site electrical distribution system, which colour plug indicates a 400 volt supply?

A Yellow

B Blue

C Black

D Red

12.22

Why should batteries **never** be stored loose in a tool bag?

A They might not be recharged

B The tool bag will be heavy and cause back injuries

C If the terminals short out, they could cause a fire

D They give off a poisonous gas in a confined space

C 12

12.23

A gang is using an insulated pick to break up a surface. What **two** hazards should they be aware of?

- [A] Standing too close to the worker with the pick
- [B] Smoking, as gas could be released
- [C] Damage to eyes caused by sunlight reflecting off the pick
- [D] Standing with their hands in their pockets
- [E] Standing in front of, or behind, the worker with the pick

12.24

A worker is using a generator to power some lighting when the lamp blows. They have a spare lamp, what should they do?

- [A] Disconnect the lighting from the generator before replacing the lamp
- [B] Wait for an electrician with a NICEIC card
- [C] Replace the lamp without disconnecting the generator, as you can't get a shock from it
- [D] Carry on working in the dark

12.25

Why is temporary continuity bonding carried out before removing and replacing sections of metallic pipework?

- [A] To provide a continuous earth for the pipework installation
- [B] To prevent any chance of blowing a fuse
- [C] To maintain the live supply to the electrical circuit
- [D] To prevent any chance of corrosion to the pipework

C
12

13 Site transport safety and lifting operations

13.01

Which of the following, by itself, provides the **best** solution for reducing risks related to site transport and access?

- A Providing all site staff with information detailing the site layout and designated traffic routes
- B A one-way traffic system complete with segregated pedestrian routes
- C Ensuring that there are adequate signs directing traffic to various parts of the site
- D Reducing the need for some vehicle movements on site by requiring more materials to be offloaded manually outside the site

13.02

Which **two** of the following conditions would you expect a site manager to apply in order to manage the risk of site staff operating plant?

- A The plant operative must be trained and competent
- B The plant operative must be authorised
- C The plant operative must be over 21 years old
- D The plant operative must hold a full driving licence
- E The plant operative must be under 65 years old

13.03

What should you do if you see a dumper being driven too fast?

- A Keep out of its way and report the matter to the site manager
- B Try to catch the dumper and speak to the driver
- C Report the matter to the Health and Safety Executive (HSE)
- D Do nothing, dumpers are allowed to go above the site speed limit

13.04

While observing an excavator digging a trial pit you notice that liquid is dripping and forming a small pool under the back of the machine. What could this mean?

- A It is normal for fluids to vent after the machine stops
- B The machine is hot so the diesel has expanded and overflowed
- C Someone put too much diesel into the machine before it started work
- D The machine may have a hydraulic fluid leak and could be unsafe

13.05

How should workers be told about the site traffic rules?

- A During site induction
- B By a Health and Safety Executive (HSE) inspector
- C By a note on the site notice or hazard board
- D By the plant operators

Answers: 13.01 = B   13.02 = A, B   13.03 = A   13.04 = D   13.05 = A

13.06

When can a mobile plant operator let people ride in, or on, the machine?

A. Only if they have a long way to go

B. Only if it is raining

C. Only if it is designed to carry passengers

D. At any time

13.07

You notice a build-up of diesel fumes in the area of the site that you are visiting. What should you do?

A. Try to turn off the piece of plant that is creating the fumes

B. Quickly inform the site manager of this hazardous situation

C. Carry out the visit quickly to minimise exposure

D. Move out of the affected area at regular intervals to get fresh air

13.08

Which of the following represents good site management on the public road approaching a site?

A. Providing a place where drivers can park delivery lorries off the road

B. Parking items of plant to free up space on site

C. Signs apologising for any inconvenience caused

D. Asking contractors to park half on the footpath and half on the road so the site entrance can be seen more easily

13.09

You see a mobile crane lifting a load that is about to hit something. What should you do?

A. Warn the site manager

B. Warn the person supervising the lift

C. Warn the crane driver

D. Do nothing and assume everything is under control

13.10

You think a load is about to fall from a moving forklift truck. What should you do?

A. Keep clear but try to warn the driver and others in the area

B. Run alongside the machine and try to hold on to the load

C. Run and tell the site manager

D. Sound the nearest fire alarm bell

13.11

What is the correct procedure for using a tower crane to offload a lorry?

A. Lorry drivers must sling the load before the trained slinger signaller arrives

B. Anyone can sling the load, providing it will not pass over people when on the crane

C. A trained slinger signaller to carry out the offloading operation

D. The crane driver to instruct an operative to sling the load

C
13

13.12

What should all lifting equipment and accessories be?

- A Brightly coloured, inspected and clearly signed
- B Regularly maintained, clean and tidy
- C Logged, inspected, thoroughly examined and marked
- D Strong enough for the load and always fitted with outriggers

13.13

You need to walk past someone using a mobile crane. What should you do?

- A Anticipate what the crane operator will do next and then pass
- B Try to catch the attention of the crane operator first
- C Walk past, but only if you are wearing Class 2 or Class 3 hi-vis clothing
- D Take another route so that you stay clear of the crane

13.14

You need to walk past a 360° mobile crane. The crane is operating near a wall. What is the **main** danger?

- A You may put the crane driver off if they suddenly see you
- B You could be crushed if you walk between the crane and the wall
- C The crane's diesel exhaust fumes could build up near the wall and become a hazard to you
- D Noise levels may increase above safe levels as they will echo off the wall

13.15

You are walking across the site. A large mobile crane reverses across your path. What should you do?

- A Help the driver to reverse
- B Start to run so that you can pass behind the reversing crane
- C Pass close to the front of the crane
- D Wait or find another way around the crane

13.16

When is site transport allowed to drive along a pedestrian route?

- A During meal breaks
- B If it is the shortest route
- C Only if necessary and if all pedestrians are excluded
- D Only if the vehicle has a flashing yellow light

13.17

How would you expect a well-organised site to keep pedestrians away from traffic routes?

- A The site manager will direct all pedestrians away from traffic routes
- B The traffic routes will be shown on the site notice or hazard board
- C There will be physical barriers between traffic and pedestrian routes
- D The plant operators will be given strict instructions on which route they must take

13.18

When is a site vehicle **most** likely to injure pedestrians?

- A While reversing
- B While lifting materials onto scaffolds
- C While tipping into an excavation
- D While digging out footings

13.19

Why must you **not** walk behind a lorry when it is reversing?

- A Most lorries are not fitted with mirrors
- B The driver is unlikely to know you are there
- C The driver may think you are the signaller
- D You could be overcome by exhaust fumes

13.20

The easiest way to the place you want to be on site is through a contractor's vehicle compound. Which route should you take?

- A Around the compound if vehicles are moving
- B Straight through the compound if no vehicles appear to be moving
- C Around the compound every time
- D Through the compound but staying close to the edge away from vehicles

13.21

A forklift truck is blocking the way to where you want to go on site. It is lifting materials on to a scaffold. What should you do?

- A Only walk under the raised load if you are wearing a safety helmet
- B Catch the driver's attention and then walk under the raised load
- C Start to run so that you are not under the load for very long
- D Wait or go around, but never walk under a raised load

13.22

Which of the following is the **most** effective way of preventing pedestrians being struck by site vehicles?

- A All vehicles must switch on their flashing amber beacon
- B Separate access gates and routes for pedestrians and vehicles
- C Hi-vis vests being worn when pedestrians walk up the site road
- D A wide site road with a good quality surface

13.23

Which of the following is the **best** risk control measure with regard to site vehicles reversing?

- A Setting a speed limit on site
- B Vehicles fitted with reversing bleepers
- C A vehicle marshaller should reverse all vehicles, especially on and off site
- D All vehicles should be fitted with CCTV to help them reverse

13.24

When you walk across the site, what is the **best** way to avoid an accident with mobile plant?

- A Keep to the designated pedestrian routes
- B Keep to the routes everyone else is taking
- C Get the attention of the driver before you get too close
- D Wear hi-vis clothing

13.25

Which of these would you **not** expect to see if site transport is well organised?

- A Speed limits
- B Barriers to keep pedestrians away from mobile plant and vehicles
- C Pedestrians and mobile plant using the same routes
- D One-way systems

13.26

How can a contractor ensure that the sequence of operations to enable a lift to be carried out safely are in place?

- A Using verbal instructions
- B Check the lift plan or method statement
- C Using a toolbox talk
- D Using a risk assessment

13.27

A crane has to do a difficult lift. The signaller asks you to help, but you are **not** trained in recognised hand signals. What should you do?

- A Politely refuse because you don't know how to signal
- B Start giving signals to the crane driver
- C Only help if the signaller really can't manage alone
- D Ask the signaller to show you what signals to use

13.28

A truck has to tip materials into a trench. Who should give signals to the truck driver?

A Anyone who is wearing a hi-vis coat

B Someone standing in the trench

C Someone who knows the signals

D Only the person who is trained and appointed for the job

D

High risk activities

Contents

14 Working at height

14.01

If someone is wearing a harness and fall-arrest lanyard while working at height, what else **must** be done?

A Provide an extra harness in case theirs breaks

B Nothing else, wearing a harness is good enough

C Have a rescue plan in place to retrieve them quickly if they fall

D Have a second person warn them if they get too close to the edge

14.02

What is the main danger of leaving someone who has fallen suspended in a harness for too long?

A The anchorage point may fail

B They may try to climb back up the structure and fall again

C They may suffer loss of consciousness or fatal injury

D It is a distraction for other workers

14.03

When is it **most** appropriate to use a safety harness and lanyard for working at height?

A Only when the roof has a steep pitch

B Only when crossing a flat roof with clear roof lights

C Only when all other options for fall prevention have been ruled out

D Only when materials are stored at height

14.04

What should a worker do if a fall-restraint lanyard has damaged stitching?

A Use the lanyard if the damaged stitching is less than 5 cm long

B Get a replacement lanyard

C Do not use the damaged lanyard and work without one

D Use the lanyard if the damaged stitching is less than 15 cm long

D
14

Answers: 14.01 = C   14.02 = C   14.03 = C   14.04 = B

14.05

In order to carry out a structural inspection a worker needs to wear a full body harness. They have **never** used one before. What **must** happen before they start work?

A Their employer must provide them with information, competent advice and training

B Ask someone wearing a similar harness to show them what to do

C Nothing, they should work it out by themselves

D Read the instruction book and follow the advice that it contains

14.06

If the airbag being used for fall arrest has a controlled leak rate, what criteria **must** the inflation pump meet?

A It must be electrically powered

B It must be switched off from time to time to avoid over-inflation

C It must run all the time while work is carried out at height

D It must be switched off when the airbags are full

14.07

Why is it dangerous to use inflatable airbags for fall arrest that are too big for the area to be protected?

A They will exert a sideways pressure on anything that is containing them

B The pressure in the bags will cause them to burst

C The inflation pump will become overloaded

D They will not fully inflate

14.08

What is the maximum permitted gap between the guard-rails on a working platform?

A 350 mm

B 470 mm

C 490 mm

D 510 mm

14.09

Under the requirements of the Work at Height Regulations, what is the minimum width of a working platform?

A Two scaffold boards wide

B Three scaffold boards wide

C Four scaffold boards wide

D Suitable and sufficient for the job in hand

D
14

14.10

What is the minimum height of the main guard-rail on a working platform?

A. 750 mm

B. 850 mm

C. 950 mm

D. 1,050 mm

14.11

The Beaufort Scale is important when working at height externally. What does it measure?

A. It measures air temperature

B. It measures the load-bearing capacity of a flat roof

C. It measures wind speed

D. It measures the load-bearing capacity of a scaffold

D
14

14.12

What is the **most effective** method of preventing workers from falling from height while carrying out construction and maintenance work?

A. Leave the decisions on how to work at height to the principal contractor

B. Ensure that details of risky operations are included in the construction phase health and safety plan

C. Educate the workforce to be more careful while working at height

D. Ensure that design and construction solutions eliminate the need for working at height

14.13

What is the **main** reason for using a safety net or other soft-landing system rather than a personal fall-arrest system?

A. Soft-landing systems are cheaper to use and do not need inspecting

B. It is always easier to rescue workers who fall into a soft-landing system

C. Specialist knowledge is not required to install soft-landing systems

D. Soft-landing systems are collective fall arrest measures

14.14

What **must** edge protection be designed to do?

A. Allow persons to work on both sides of it

B. Secure tools and materials close to the edge

C. Warn people where the edge of the roof is

D. Prevent people and materials from falling

14.15

In law you are working at height when you fall from what height?

A. Any height that would cause an injury if you fell

B. 2 m above the ground or higher

C. 3 m above the ground or higher

D. The first lift of a scaffold or higher

Answers: 14.10 = C   14.11 = C   14.12 = D   14.13 = D   14.14 = D   14.15 = A

14.16

Following the hierarchy of control, which of the following is regarded as the **last resort** for someone's safety when working at height?

- A. Safety harness and fall arrest lanyard
- B. Safety netting or airbags
- C. Mobile elevating work platform (MEWP)
- D. Mobile access tower

14.17

What is the **best** way to make sure that a ladder is secure and won't slip?

- A. Ensure that it is tied at the top
- B. Ask someone to stand with their foot on the bottom rung
- C. Tie it at the bottom
- D. Ask for the bottom of the ladder to be wedged with blocks of wood

14.18

To ensure the safety of people who have to gain access to a place of work at height, how should you regard ladders?

- A. They are always acceptable for work below 2 m
- B. You can use them if it gets the job done more quickly
- C. They are generally the least favoured form of access equipment
- D. They are now banned on all sites

14.19

How far should a ladder extend above the stepping-off point if there is no alternative, firm handhold?

- A. Two rungs
- B. Three rungs
- C. Half a metre
- D. Five rungs or one metre

14.20

When using portable or pole ladders for access, what is the maximum vertical distance between landings?

- A. 2 m
- B. 5 m
- C. 9 m
- D. 30 m

14.21

What is a Class 3 ladder?

- A. A ladder for domestic use only and must not be used on site
- B. An industrial quality ladder which can be used safely
- C. A ladder that is made of wood
- D. It is made of insulating material and can be used near to overhead cables

D
14

14.22

When using a leaning ladder what should the slope or angle of the ladder be?

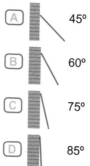

A) 45°

B) 60°

C) 75°

D) 85°

14.23

To ensure your safety when carrying out an inspection at height, who must erect mobile tower scaffolds?

A) Someone who has the instruction book

B) Someone who is trained, competent and authorised

C) Advanced scaffolders

D) A worker of the hire company

D 14

14.24

As part of a feasibility study you are planning an inspection of roof trusses inside a factory building. What is the recommended **maximum** height for a free-standing mobile tower when used indoors?

A) There is no height restriction

B) Three lifts

C) As specified by the manufacturer

D) Three times the longest base dimension

14.25

After gaining access to the platform of a mobile tower, what is the **first** thing you should do?

A) Check that the tower's brakes are locked on

B) Check that the tower has been correctly assembled

C) Close the access hatch to stop people or equipment from falling

D) Check that the tower does not rock or wobble

14.26

An outdoor tower scaffold has stood overnight in high winds and heavy rain. What should you ensure before the scaffold is used?

A) That the brakes still work

B) That the scaffold is tied to the adjacent structure

C) That the scaffold is inspected by a competent person

D) That the platform hatch still works correctly

Answers: 14.22 = C   14.23 = B   14.24 = C   14.25 = C   14.26 = C

14.27

A person is going to be working on a mobile tower but will **not** be erecting, altering or dismantling it. What training should they have?

- [A] They need the same level of training as a person erecting, altering or dismantling it
- [B] They do not need any training
- [C] They should be briefed on the safe use and hazards of working on a mobile tower
- [D] They should read the manufacturer's instructions

14.28

How will you know the maximum weight or number of people that can be lifted safely on a mobile elevating work platform (MEWP)?

- [A] The weight limit is reached when the platform is full
- [B] It will say on the Health and Safety Law poster
- [C] You will be told during site induction
- [D] From an information plate fixed to the machine

14.29

When is it safe to use a mobile elevating work platform (MEWP) on soft ground?

- [A] When the ground is dry
- [B] When the machine can stand on scaffold planks laid over the soft ground
- [C] When ground load bearing capacity has been assessed as suitable
- [D] When it is fitted with outriggers

14.30

What should someone working from a cherry picker attach their lanyard to?

- [A] A strong part of the structure that they are working on
- [B] A designated anchorage point inside the platform
- [C] A secure point on the boom of the machine
- [D] A scaffold guard-rail

D
14

14.31

A mobile elevating work platform (MEWP) is being used to carry out work at height. What is the **only** circumstance, in normal use, in which it is acceptable to lower the platform using the ground-level controls?

A When the person using the ground-level controls is competent to do so

B In an emergency

C If the person working on the platform needs to step off the MEWP to gain access to the high-level work area

D If the person working on the platform needs both hands free to carry out their job

14.32

You have to carry out an inspection at height, using a cherry picker. When would you **not** clip yourself to the machine using a restraint lanyard?

A For any type of roof work

B When you are working over, or near to deep water

C When you are climbing from the machine on to the structure

D When you are standing on the mid guard-rail to carry out the inspection

14.33

What is a common example of a fragile roof material?

A Asphalt felt roof

B Asbestos cement sheets

C Raised seam roofs

D Single-ply membrane

14.34

You are inspecting a flat roof. What is the **best** way to stop yourself and others from falling over the edge?

A Have a large warning sign placed at the edge of the roof

B Ask someone to keep watch and to shout out when someone gets too close to the edge

C Ask for the edge to be protected with a guard-rail and toe-boards

D Ask for red and white tape to mark the edge

14.35

What is the **best** way to stop people falling through voids, holes or fragile roof panels?

A Tell everyone where the dangerous areas are

B Covers, secured in place, that can take the weight of a person and add warning signage

C Cover them with netting

D Mark the areas with red and white tape

D 14

Answers: 14.31 = B   14.32 = B   14.33 = B   14.34 = C   14.35 = B

14.36

 What does this sign mean?

A Load bearing roof. You can stand on the surface but not on any roof lights

B Fragile roof. Take care when walking on roof surface

C Fragile roof. Do not stand directly on roof and use fall protection measures

D Load-bearing roof. Surface can be slippery when wet

14.37

To ensure your safety and that of the site workers, what should a contractor include in a safety method statement for working at height? Give **three** answers.

A The cost of the job and time it will take

B The sequence of operations and the equipment to be used

C How much insurance cover will be required

D How falls are to be prevented

E Who will supervise the job on site

14.38

When work is being carried out above public areas what should be your **first** consideration?

A To minimise the number of people below at any one time

B To provide alternative routes for the public and keep them away from the area

C To let the public know what you are doing

D To provide netting to prevent falling objects

14.39

Which of the following provides the public with adequate protection from falling objects?

A Clear warning signs

B A worker in a hi-vis vest standing on the footway to warn people

C Viewing panels in the site hoarding

D A fan or scaffold tunnel over the footway

**D
14**

14.40

Which of these statements about work at height is **true**?

A It must be risk assessed and properly planned

B It must only be undertaken by scaffold contractors

C It must be carried out as quickly as possible

D It must be suspended if the forecast wind speed is above Force 2

14.41

How should access be controlled, if people are working in a riser shaft?

A By a site security operative

B By those who are working in it

C By the main contractor

D By a permit to work system

14.42

You are working at height taking site measurements, but the securing cord for a safety net is in your way. What should you do?

A Untie the cord, carry out your work and tie it up again

B Untie the cord, but ask the contractor to re-tie it when you have finished

C Tell the contractor that you are going to untie the cord

D Leave the cord alone and report the problem to the contractor

14.43

While carrying out a site visit you see someone who is working above a damaged safety net system. What should you do?

A Ask them to work somewhere away from the damaged area of net

B Ask them to stop work and report it to the site manager

C Ask them to tie the damaged edges together using the net test cords

D Ask them to go and see if they can get hold of a harness and lanyard

14.44

A scaffold guard-rail **must** be removed to allow a worker to carry out a survey. The worker is **not** a scaffolder. Can they remove the guard-rail?

A Yes, if they put it back as soon as they have finished

B Yes, if they put it back before they leave site

C No, only a scaffolder can remove the guard-rail but any worker can put it back

D No, only a scaffolder can remove the guard-rail and put it back

14.45

To ensure safety when using a scaffold to carry out work at height, when must a competent person routinely inspect the scaffold?

A Before it is first used and then at intervals not exceeding seven days

B Only after it has been erected

C After it has been erected and then at monthly intervals

D After it has been erected and then at intervals not exceeding 10 days

D
14

Answers: 14.41 = D   14.42 = D   14.43 = B   14.44 = D   14.45 = A

14.46

When can someone who is **not** a scaffolder adapt an independent scaffold?

- A If the scaffold is not more than two lifts in height
- B As long as a scaffolder refits the parts after the work has finished
- C Never, only trained scaffolders can modify scaffolding
- D Only if it is a tube and fittings scaffolding

14.47

You need to use a ladder to get to a scaffold platform. Which **one** of these statements is true?

- A It must be tied and extend 1 m or five rungs above the platform
- B All broken rungs must be clearly marked
- C It must be wedged at the bottom to stop it slipping
- D Two people must be on the ladder at all times to provide stability

14.48

How do you identify the safe load rating for a scaffold platform?

- A Ask the site manager
- B Ask the telehandler driver
- C The safe load is breached when the ledgers start to deflect
- D Refer to the handover certificate or signage

14.49

A scaffold has to be erected to remove asbestos. What action does the scaffolder **not** need to take?

- A Apply to the HSE for an ancillary license for asbestos work
- B Provide a separate notice to the HSE for the works where asbestos is present
- C Send employees for a health survey if the exposure level is below the threshold
- D Provide a scaffold handover certificate

14.50

What is the **maximum** recommended gap between a scaffold and the structure?

- A No greater than 225 mm
- B No greater than 300 mm
- C No greater than 470 mm
- D No greater than 600 mm

14.51

What action should be taken **before** using a scaffold which is secured by masonry anchors?

- A There must be an inspection tag in place marked with the current date
- B Ties must have been counted
- C Ties must have been tested by a competent person
- D The scaffolder must have been consulted

D
14

14.52

Why should a ladder never be painted?

A The paint will make the rungs slippery

B The paint may hide any damaged parts

C The paint could damage the metal parts of the ladder

D It will need regular re-painting

D
14

Answers: 14.52 = B

15 Excavations and confined spaces

15.01

You are in a deep trench and start to feel dizzy. What is the **first** thing you should do?

- A Ask others if they feel dizzy. If they don't then carry on for five minutes
- B Have a drink, it's the first sign of dehydration
- C Make sure that you and any others get out quickly and report it
- D Sit down, put your head between your knees and take deep breaths to get some oxygen back into your system

15.02

Which of these is **not** a hazard in a confined space?

- A Toxic gas
- B A lack of carbon dioxide
- C A lack of oxygen
- D Flammable or explosive gas

15.03

Give **two** reasons why methane gas is dangerous in confined spaces.

- A It can explode
- B It makes you hyperactive
- C You will not be able to see because of the dense fumes
- D It makes you dehydrated
- E You may not have enough oxygen to breathe

15.04

What might happen if the level of oxygen drops below 8% in a confined space?

- A Your hearing could be affected
- B There is a high risk of fire or explosion
- C You could become unconscious
- D You might get dehydrated

15.05

You are working in a confined space when you notice the smell of bad eggs. What is this a sign of?

- A Hydrogen sulphide
- B Oxygen
- C Methane
- D Carbon dioxide

D
15

15.06

What should you do if you are in a confined space when the gas alarm sounds?

A Switch off the alarm

B Get out of the confined space immediately

C Carry on working but do not use electrical tools

D Carry on working but take plenty of breaks in the fresh air

15.07

As part of a site survey you are required to work in a confined space. How should the air be checked?

A Unsafe atmospheres have a particular odour so someone should go in and smell the air

B No-one should enter until the air has been tested with the appropriate gas detection monitor

C Warning signs will indicate the presence of an unsafe atmosphere

D Unsafe atmospheres have little oxygen so the air should be tested with a flame to see if it stays alight

15.08

What danger is created by excessive oxygen in a confined space?

A Increase in breathing rate of workers

B Combustible materials are more likely to catch fire

C Decreased working time inside work area

D False sense of security

15.09

What do guard-rails around the top of an excavation prevent?

A Heavy plant from toppling into the excavation

B People from falling into the trench and being injured

C The sides of the trench from collapsing

D Material from spoil heaps falling into the excavation

15.10

You are standing near a deep trench. A lorry backs up to the trench and the engine is left running. What should you do?

A Put on ear defenders to cut out the engine noise

B Ignore it, the lorry will soon drive away

C Look to see if there is a toxic gas meter in the trench

D Get everyone out of the trench quickly

15.11

When should an excavation be battered back or stepped?

A If it is more than 5 m deep

B If there is water in the bottom of the trench

C If there is a risk of the sides falling in, regardless of depth

D If any buried services cross the excavation

D
15

Answers: 15.06 = B   15.07 = B   15.08 = B   15.09 = B   15.10 = D   15.11 = C

15.12

If you see the side supports of an excavation move, what should you do **first**?

- A Keep watching to see if they move again
- B Make sure that everyone working in the excavation gets out quickly
- C Do nothing as slight movement in the supports is quite normal
- D Move the workers to another part of the excavation

15.13

What is a significant hazard when excavating alongside a building or structure?

- A Undermining or weakening the foundations of the building
- B Noise and vibration affecting the occupiers of the building
- C Ground water entering the excavation
- D Damaging the surface finish of the building

15.14

When should you take precautions to prevent people, materials, or equipment from falling into an excavation?

- A At all times
- B When the excavation is 2 m or more deep
- C When more than five people are working in the excavation
- D When there is a risk from an underground cable or other service

15.15

How should dumpers be prevented from falling into or damaging the edge of an excavation?

- A Dumpers kept 5 m away from the excavation
- B Stop blocks provided, parallel to the trench, appropriate to the vehicle's wheel size
- C Dumper drivers required to judge the distance carefully or given stop signals by another person
- D Cones or signage erected to indicate safe tipping point

15.16

Which of these is the **most** accurate way to confirm the exact location of buried services?

- A Existing service drawings
- B Trial holes
- C Survey drawings
- D Architect drawings

D
15

15.17

Which piece of equipment may need to be used with a cable avoidance tool (CAT) in order to detect cables?

- A Insulated shovel or spade
- B Signal generator (genny)
- C Excavator bucket with no teeth
- D Gas detector

15.18

What **must** happen each time before a shift starts work in an excavation?

A. The workers should tighten any loose supports

B. A competent person must inspect the excavation

C. The workers should go down and pump out any rainwater

D. The workers should go down and check that everything is OK and report back to the supervisor

15.19

What is the **safest** way to get into and out of a deep excavation?

A. Use an excavator bucket

B. Use the buried services as steps

C. Use the shoring or trench supports

D. Use a fixed staircase

15.20

What is one duty of the top man if you need to work in a confined space?

A. To tell you how to work safely in confined spaces

B. To enter the confined space if there is a problem

C. To start the rescue plan if needed

D. To supervise the work in the confined space

15.21

What is the **best** way to avoid the potential for someone becoming trapped in an excavation?

A. Eliminate the need for anyone to go into it

B. Check the contractor's method statement

C. Review the last excavation inspection record

D. Go down in a cage suspended from a crane

15.22

What is the **first** question to ask if work may need to be carried out in a confined space?

A. Can it be undertaken by someone else

B. Can it be avoided

C. Can it be managed by limiting the amount of time people are in it

D. Can it be controlled with radios or mobile phones

15.23

Work in a confined space usually needs a risk assessment, a method statement and what other safety document?

A. A permit to enter

B. An up to date staff handbook

C. A written contract for the work

D. A company health and safety policy

D
15

15.24

You are required to undertake a survey in what you suspect might be a confined space. What should be your **first** consideration?

- A   Make sure that you have the correct equipment to test the atmosphere
- B   Make sure that you have a colleague with you
- C   Check if the information you need can be obtained remotely to avoid entering the space
- D   Follow a safe system of work for entering the confined space, including emergency arrangements

15.25

You are arranging for an inspection in a confined space to be carried out. Which are the **two** most important safety requirements?

- A   Completing a permit to work form
- B   Informing your office before entering
- C   Entering slowly and breathing shallowly until you are sure the air is good to breathe
- D   Ensuring that a safe system of work has been identified and is followed
- E   Making sure that emergency rescue arrangements are in place

15.26

What should be the **first** consideration of the contractor's responsible person before planning for anyone to enter a confined space?

- A   Has the atmosphere in the confined space been tested
- B   Has a safe means of access and egress been established
- C   Is there an alternative method of doing the work
- D   Has everyone who intends to enter the confined space been properly trained

D
15

D
15

E

Environment

Contents

16 Environmental awareness and waste control

16.01

Under environmental law, which statement is **true**?

A. Only directors can be prosecuted if they do not follow the law

B. Only companies can be prosecuted if they do not follow the law

C. Only employees can be prosecuted if they do not follow the law

D. Companies and employees can be prosecuted if they do not follow the law

16.02

A bird is discovered on a nest in an area where work is to take place. What should you do?

A. Cover it with a bucket

B. Move it, do your work and then put it back

C. Protect the nest and seek specialist advice on how to proceed

D. Scare it away

16.03

What is the legal duty of the site manager when an invasive species of plant, such as Japanese knotweed, is discovered on site?

A. To ensure it is transplanted to a part of the site where it will not be disturbed in the future

B. To prevent the spread of the plant in the wild

C. To inform the Health and Safety Executive (HSE) of its presence

D. To leave it undisturbed as it is protected by law

16.04

You become aware that an active bird's nest has been destroyed on your site. Which of the following is a possible outcome?

A. A visit from an RSPCA inspector

B. A prohibition notice issued by the Health and Safety Executive (HSE)

C. Prosecution by the RSPB

D. A caution or prosecution by the police wildlife crime officer

E
16

Answers: 16.01 = D   16.02 = C   16.03 = B   16.04 = D

16.05

If you find bats on site, which of the following statements is **true**?

A Bats are not a protected species so you can disturb or destroy their shelters or resting places

B You can move the shelters or resting places of bats as long as you do it at night when they are out hunting

C You can disturb or destroy shelters or resting places of bats if they get in the way of building work

D All bat species and their roosts are protected, you cannot disturb them without licensed mitigation

16.06

What should you do if you see a large volume of material stored under a tree?

A Nothing, materials can be stored anywhere

B Ensure that the material is removed if the tree looks damaged

C Ensure that the material is removed and tree protection fencing is placed around the tree to prevent further damage

D Ensure that the tree is watered regularly until the materials are removed

16.07

Why is energy efficiency important?

A It can help to mitigate the rising costs of energy

B To comply with UK legislation and carbon reduction targets

C To help reduce climate change and the impact carbon emissions and other pollutants have on the environment

D All of these answers

16.08

Which of the following does **not** help save energy and resources on site?

A Use of alternative or recycled products for site set-up, logistics and enabling works

B Installation of more energy efficient site accommodation and adoption of low energy technology for site and task lighting

C Ensuring the site connects to the electricity supply as early as possible to avoid running on fuel powered generators

D Use of cheaper products and materials to reduce costs

E
16

16.09

You are planning a site's power set-up. Which of the following is the **most** energy efficient?

A) A diesel powered generator

B) A gas powered generator

C) A combination of solar power and mains power

D) Mains electricity

16.10

The future use or energy performance of a building or structure can be affected if it is not built correctly. You notice a detail can't be built as it has been designed. What should you do?

A) Instruct the tradesperson to build the detail as best they can

B) Make sure the issue is raised with the person responsible for the design

C) Substitute the detail with components which could work without consulting the person responsible for the design

D) Use your experience and build it as you think it should be done

16.11

You are considering using an alternative material or component to that specified. What is often overlooked?

A) The impact of the alternative on the building or structure's future energy performance

B) The cost of the alternative, which is often much lower than the material normally used

C) Whether the alternative is readily available

D) Whether the alternative will look similar to the product specified

16.12

What are you liable to pay landfill tax on?

A) On waste sent for energy recovery

B) On waste that is reused

C) On waste that is landfilled

D) On waste that is recycled

16.13

You are aware that a job has resulted in some plasterboard off-cuts. Can these go in with the general waste?

A) Yes, because plasterboard is not hazardous waste

B) Yes, because the boards will only be a small proportion of the skip content

C) No, because plasterboard is hazardous waste

D) No, because plasterboard should not be mixed with other wastes

E
16

16.14

Someone has turned up at the site and offered to take your surplus soil away for free. Which of the following is **not** a legal requirement?

- A They are a registered waste carrier
- B They are able to complete a duty of care note
- C They have got a clean driving licence
- D They will take the soil to an authorised site

16.15

Can waste electronic and electrical equipment (WEEE) be disposed of with other wastes?

- A Only if it is put in scrap metal skips
- B No, WEEE must be disposed of separately
- C Yes, in a general waste skip providing there are no more than three items
- D Only if it is mixed with other hazardous waste

16.16

What duty of care documentation should you use for hazardous waste leaving your site?

- A A waste transfer note with a written description of the waste and transferor details
- B A hazardous waste consignment note that includes details of the disposal or treatment facility
- C None, as long as the carrier is registered and has a waste carrier's licence
- D A skip ticket that includes the vehicle registration number and waste carrier details

16.17

A skip-lorry driver hands you a copy of the Hazardous Waste Consignment Note with Section C (carrier's details) signed. If you are responsible for the waste, what is the **first** thing you need to do with it?

- A Refuse to take the note as you do not need a copy
- B Take the note and file it for future reference
- C Check that the details in Sections A, B and C are correct before you sign Section D (producer's details)
- D As the waste is on his truck it is not your responsibility to sign the note

E
16

Answers: 16.14 = C   16.15 = B   16.16 = B   16.17 = C

16.18

What final element is missing from this simple four point pollution incident response plan?

Stop – Contain – Notify – ?

A. Review
B. Clean up
C. Take action
D. Re-start work

16.19

When assessing pollution risk, before starting works on a construction site, which of the following should **not** be done?

A. Locate and identify watercourses, surface water and foul water drains
B. Seal up all drains and gullies on site
C. Evaluate the risk of pollution entering existing drains and watercourses during the works
D. Inspect existing gullies, silt traps and oil separators

16.20

Which **three** of the following are possible pollution risks that could result from excavation activities?

A. Dust
B. Contaminated soils
C. Pumping out of silty water
D. Work at height
E. Disturbing protected species

16.21

Which **two** of the following should be undertaken to help improve a pollution incident response?

A. Train workforce in the use of spill kits
B. Always refuel using drip trays
C. Practise the incident response by undertaking mock exercises
D. Train one responsible person in the use of spill kits
E. Only use biodegradable fuels

16.22

The programme of works you are managing has run behind and you will need the site to be operational on a Sunday. The operations will be noisy and there are nearby residents. What action should you take before working?

A. Ensure the site operations are only done during daylight hours
B. Inform the residents in writing that you will be working on Sunday and that it could be noisy
C. Apply for permission from the local environmental health officer under a Section 61 notice
D. Do not work, you can never work on a Sunday

E 16

16.23

What **two** precautions should be taken to reduce the risk of water pollution when mixing concrete and cement on site?

- A It should be at least 5 m from a watercourse
- B It should be at least 10 m from a watercourse
- C It should be sited on an impermeable area
- D It should not be allowed on site if water pollution is a possibility
- E It should only be used under the direct supervision of the site manager

16.24

Which **two** of the following will help to minimise dust from stockpiles of soil?

- A Avoid moving materials when nearby residents are at home
- B Damping down the materials with water
- C Seed the stockpile
- D Regularly move or mix materials between stockpiles
- E Have a supply of face masks suitable for nuisance dust

16.25

To prevent pollution to watercourses what would be the **best** solution to control surface water run-off from material stockpiles?

- A Directing the water run-off away from the watercourse to the nearest surface water drain
- B Channelling the water run-off directly into the foul water sewer
- C Installing silt fence around the stockpile
- D Making sure stockpiles are more than 215 m away from watercourses

16.26

Which of the following are **two** environmental reasons for preventing concrete, screed or mortar washout water from entering watercourses or underground aquifers?

- A It can change the colour of the water
- B It can change the pH balance of the water
- C It will improve the flow of the watercourse
- D It will pollute the water and could harm water wildlife
- E It may be part of the conditions of contract and a client requirement

16.27

A plant refuelling point is to be set up on a new site. Which of the following is the preferred method of fuel transfer?

- A Decanting from jerry cans using a funnel
- B Gravity feed from a bulk storage tank
- C Siphon the fuel by mouth
- D Pumped system with a nozzle fitted with an auto cut-off device

16.28

 A full 200-litre drum carrying this symbol has toppled over and the whole content has seeped into the ground. Which of the following agencies should be informed?

- A The Health and Safety Executive (HSE)
- B The EU Authority on Chemical Safety
- C The Environment Agency in England, SEPA in Scotland or Natural Resources in Wales
- D The Health Protection Agency

16.29

What should be the capacity of a spillage bund around a fuel storage tank, in addition to the volume of content of the tank?

- A 10% (110% of the total content)
- B 30% (130% of the total content)
- C 50% (150% of the total content)
- D 75% (175% of the total content)

E
16

F

Specialist activities

Contents

The following specialist activities are included within the managers and professionals test and **all** need to be revised.

17 Construction (Design and Management) Regulations

17.01

Under the Construction (Design and Management) Regulations 2015, who is responsible for providing pre-construction information?

- [A] The contractor
- [B] The client
- [C] The designer
- [D] The principal contractor

17.02

According to the Construction (Design and Management) Regulations 2015, what must a contractor have before they can be appointed on a project?

- [A] A copy of the Construction (Design and Management) Regulations 2015
- [B] A relevant competency card
- [C] Sufficient resources to enable them to fulfil their regulatory duties
- [D] The necessary skills, knowledge and experience to do the work

17.03

Under the Construction (Design and Management) Regulations 2015, who must make suitable arrangements for managing a project, including the allocation of sufficient time and other resources?

- [A] The principal designer
- [B] The client
- [C] The contractor
- [D] The designer

17.04

Under the Construction (Design and Management) Regulations 2015, when **must** the principal contractor make arrangements for drawing up a construction phase plan?

- [A] When the project is notifiable
- [B] If the client requires one
- [C] If it is a contractual requirement
- [D] Before setting up the construction site

17.05

Under the Construction (Design and Management) Regulations 2015, what, in addition to applying the general principles of prevention, **must** a designer take into account when preparing a design?

- [A] All risk assessments on site
- [B] Nothing; the principal contractor should manage all risk
- [C] Any pre-construction information
- [D] How to secure the site

Answers: 17.01 = B   17.02 = D   17.03 = B   17.04 = D   17.05 = C

17.06

Under the Construction (Design and Management) Regulations 2015, who **must** plan, manage and monitor health and safety during the construction phase on projects with more than one contractor?

A The principal designer

B The principal contractor

C The contractor

D The designer

17.07

You are about to carry out refurbishment works on a structure which was constructed after the introduction of the Construction (Design and Management) Regulations. In which **one** of the following areas are you most likely to find relevant information for the initial development of pre-construction information?

A The construction phase plan

B The original project specification

C The fire safety plan

D The original health and safety file

17.08

Under the Construction (Design and Management) Regulations 2015, when there is only one contractor working on a project who must take the general principles of prevention into account?

A The principal designer and the client

B Designers and the principal contractor

C The principal designer

D Designers and the contractor

17.09

Under the Construction (Design and Management) Regulations 2015, what **must** contractors and designers check before they start work?

A That they have each had sufficient training

B That the principal contractor has a health and safety management system

C That the Health and Safety Executive (HSE) is notified about the project

D That the client is aware of their duties

F
1

17.10

You are contractor on a project that is notifiable under the Construction (Design and Management) Regulations 2015 but you have not seen an F10. What should you do?

A. Ensure that the client is aware of their duty to submit an F10

B. Work to the client's brief

C. Complete all your work within your brief and ignore the lack of F10 notification

D. Submit an F10 to the Health and Safety Executive (HSE) yourself

17.11

Under the Construction (Design and Management) Regulations 2015, what is **one** of the purposes of the health and safety file?

A. To provide pre-construction information for any future work to be carried out on the structure

B. To collate construction phase plans, risk assessments and method statements

C. To record the health and safety performance of the project during the construction phase

D. To collate contract documentation and statistics

17.12

Under the Construction (Design and Management) Regulations 2015, where would you find details of the health and safety arrangements for managing the construction phase?

A. In the pre-construction information

B. In the client brief

C. In the construction phase plan

D. In the health and safety file

17.13

Under the Construction (Design and Management) Regulations 2015, which of the following documents **must** the principal contractor and contractor keep under review?

A. The health and safety file

B. The designer's risk assessments

C. The project programme

D. The construction phase plan

17.14

Under the Construction (Design and Management) Regulations 2015, what must contractors provide to all workers under their control?

A. Appropriate supervision, instruction and information

B. A copy of the pre-construction information

C. Confirmation of their working hours and rest breaks

D. A copy of the F10 notification

F
17

Answers: 17.10 = A   17.11 = A   17.12 = C   17.13 = D   17.14 = A

17.15

Under the Construction (Design and Management) Regulations 2015, what must be recorded in writing **before** any demolition or dismantling begins?

A The revised information for the health and safety file

B The arrangements for carrying out the demolition or dismantling

C The demolition or dismantling specification

D The pre-tender demolition or dismantling health and safety plan

17.16

Under the Construction (Design and Management) Regulations 2015, who must the principal designer pass the health and safety file to **on completion** of the construction project?

A The principal contractor

B The client

C The Health and Safety Executive (HSE)

D The designer

17.17

Under the Construction (Design and Management) Regulations 2015, which **two** of the following must be in place before work begins on site?

A A health and safety file

B Adequate welfare facilities

C A method statement

D A construction contract agreement

E Boundaries or suitable barriers to prevent unauthorised access

17.18

Under the Construction (Design and Management) Regulations 2015, who is responsible for notifying the relevant enforcing authority when a project is notifiable?

A The principal designer

B The designer

C The client

D The principal contractor

17.19

What is the **main** role of the principal designer under the Construction (Design and Management) Regulations 2015?

A To plan, manage, monitor and co-ordinate the pre-construction phase

B To ensure adequate welfare facilities are provided

C To ensure that relevant pre-construction information is included in the construction phase plan

D To monitor health and safety standards throughout the construction phase

Answers: 17.15 = B   17.16 = B   17.17 = B, E   17.18 = C   17.19 = A

17.20

Under the Construction (Design and Management) Regulations 2015, under which **one** of the following circumstances would a project become notifiable?

- [A] Where the work will last longer than 30 days and have more than 20 workers working simultaneously at any point on the project
- [B] Where the building and construction work will last more than 300 person-days
- [C] Where the work will last more than 30 days and have more than five workers working simultaneously at any point on the project
- [D] Where the work will be done by more than 30 people or last more than 500 hours

17.21

Under the Construction (Design and Management) Regulations 2015, which **two** of the following must you ensure workers have received before they start working on site?

- [A] A suitable site induction that is specific to the site and to their work
- [B] Details of the client brief and project expectations
- [C] Confirmation of their working hours and rest breaks
- [D] Details of the designer's plan of work
- [E] Information about relevant hazards and control measures

17.22

What has to be displayed on a construction site where a project is notifiable under the requirements of the Construction (Design and Management) Regulations 2015?

- [A] Notice of application to erect hoardings
- [B] Notice of the principal contractor's health and safety policy
- [C] Form F10 or a notice carrying the specified information
- [D] A statement by the client

17.23

In accordance with the Construction (Design and Management) Regulations 2015, under normal circumstances, what written information must a principal contractor make available to workers or their representatives upon request?

- [A] Information for the purpose of bringing a legal proceeding concerning health, safety and welfare
- [B] Information relating to workers' health, safety and welfare
- [C] Information relating specifically to an individual's health
- [D] Information which would be against the interests of national security concerning health, safety and welfare

17.24

Under the Construction (Design and Management) Regulations 2015, what is **not** a duty of the principal contractor when consulting and engaging with workers?

- A. Involving the workforce in matters of health and safety at work
- B. Consulting and engaging with the workforce to ensure that measures for their health and safety at work are developed
- C. Providing access and the ability to make copies of information which may affect their health, safety and welfare
- D. Sharing information regarding an individual's health and safety performance

17.25

Under the Construction (Design and Management) Regulations 2015, who has responsibility for ensuring arrangements are in place to provide welfare facilities before any person carries out construction work?

- A. The designer
- B. The principal designer
- C. The Health and Safety Executive (HSE)
- D. The client

17.26

Under the Construction (Design and Management) Regulations 2015, in which of the following situations would a principal contractor need to focus on good contractor co-operation?

- A. When a final year apprentice is carrying out a task for which they have been trained, and have completed on this site many times before
- B. When a team of roofers are working close to a bricklaying gang to complete some urgent work
- C. When the client visits site to check progress
- D. When a groundworks contractor starts on site at the beginning of the construction phase

17.27

Under the Construction (Design and Management) Regulations 2015, which **two** of the following must the contractor consider in order to provide workers under their control with appropriate supervision?

- A. The number of client and designer representatives based on site
- B. The skills, knowledge, training and experience of the workers
- C. The level of the workers' safety awareness, education, physical agility, literacy and attitude
- D. How many days the project will last
- E. Whether the work is for a domestic or commercial client

17.28

When do the Construction (Design and Management) Regulations 2015 require a supported or battered excavation to be inspected?

(A) Every seven days

(B) At the start of the shift

(C) Once a month

(D) When it is more than 2 m deep

17.29

Under the Construction (Design and Management) Regulations 2015, how long must you keep inspection records?

(A) For three months after the inspection has been carried out

(B) For one week on site, before sending them to head office

(C) Until the project is completed and then for three months

(D) Until the project is completed

18 Demolition

18.01

If there are any doubts about a building's stability, who should a demolition contractor consult?

- A. Another demolition contractor
- B. A structural engineer
- C. A Health and Safety Executive (HSE) factory inspector
- D. The company safety adviser

18.02

Which of the following does **not** ensure good health and safety standards on a demolition project?

- A. Ensuring methodologies used on site follow the contractor's method statement requirements
- B. Selecting a competent demolition contractor
- C. Ensuring the contractor has a licence to remove asbestos
- D. Ensuring task and area specific inductions are carried out

18.03

Who must be the **first** person a demolition contractor appoints before undertaking demolition operations?

- A. A competent person to supervise the work
- B. A sub-contractor to strip out the buildings
- C. A safety officer to check on health and safety compliance
- D. A quantity surveyor to price the extras

18.04

What action should be taken if the contractor discovers unlabelled drums or containers on site?

- A. They should be put in the nearest waste skip
- B. They should be ignored as they will get flattened during the demolition
- C. Work should be stopped until they have been safely dealt with
- D. They should be opened to check if the contents are flammable

18.05

What is the most common source of high levels of lead in the atmosphere during demolition work of an old building?

- A. Cold cutting lead-covered cable
- B. Stripping lead sheeting
- C. Cold cutting fuel tanks
- D. Hot cutting coated steel

F
18

18.06

After exposure to lead, what precautions should you take before eating or drinking?

A Wash your hands and face

B Do not smoke

C Change out of dirty clothes

D Rinse your mouth with clean water

18.07

When asbestos material is suspected in buildings to be demolished, what is the **first** priority?

A A competent person carries out an asbestos survey

B Notify the Health and Safety Executive (HSE) of the possible presence of asbestos

C Remove and dispose of the asbestos

D Employ a licensed asbestos remover

18.08

What do the letters SWL stand for?

A Satisfactory working limit

B Safe working level

C Satisfactory weight limit

D Safe working load

18.09

Which of the following is **true** in relation to the safe working load of a piece of equipment?

A It must never be exceeded

B It is a guide figure that may be exceeded slightly

C It may be exceeded by 10% only

D It gives half the maximum weight to be lifted

18.10

What should be clearly marked on all lifting accessories?

A Date of manufacture

B Name of maker

C Date next test is due

D Safe working load

18.11

What action should be taken by the contractor if a wire rope sling is defective?

A They should not use it and make sure that no-one else can

B They should only use it for up to half its safe working load

C They should report the defect at the end of the day

D They should only use it for small lifts under 1 tonne

F
8

Answers: 18.06 = A   18.07 = A   18.08 = D   18.09 = A   18.10 = D   18.11 = A

18.12

What safety feature is provided by FOPS on mobile plant?

- A The speed is limited when tracking over hard surfaces
- B The machine stops automatically if the operator lets go of the controls
- C The operator is protected from falling objects
- D The reach is limited when working near to live overhead cables

18.13

What should a contractor do if they discover underground services **not** previously identified?

- A Fill in the hole
- B Stop work until the situation has been resolved
- C Cut the pipe or cable to see if it's live
- D Get the machine driver to dig it out

18.14

Which is the safest method of demolishing brick or internal walls by hand?

- A Undercut the wall at ground level
- B Work across in even courses from the ceiling down
- C Work from the doorway at full height
- D Cut down at corners and collapse in sections

18.15

Who should be consulted before demolition is carried out near to overhead cables?

- A The Health and Safety Executive (HSE)
- B The fire service
- C The electricity supply company
- D The land owner

18.16

Where would you find out the method for controlling identified hazards on a demolition project?

- A The demolition toolbox talk
- B The health and safety file
- C The pre-tender health and safety plan
- D The construction phase plan

18.17

What should be obtained before safely carrying out the demolition cutting of fuel tanks?

- A A gas free certificate
- B An isolation certificate
- C An environmental assessment
- D A COSHH assessment

F
18

18.18

Which **two** of the following documents refer to the specific hazards associated with demolition work in confined spaces?

- A Safety policy
- B Permit to work
- C Risk assessment
- D Scaffolding permit
- E Hot-work permit

18.19

When do the Construction (Design and Management) Regulations require an excavation to be inspected by a competent person?

- A Every seven days
- B At the start of the shift when work is to be carried out
- C Once a month
- D When it is more than 2 m deep

F
18

19 Highway works

19.01

What should the site manager do to increase the safety of private motorists if transport leaving site is likely to deposit mud on the public road?

A Have someone in the road to slow down the traffic

B Employ an on-site method of washing the wheels of site transport

C Employ a mechanical road sweeper

D Have someone hosing down the mud in the road

19.02

Why is it **not** safe to use diesel to prevent asphalt sticking to the bed of lorries?

A It will create a slipping hazard

B It will corrode the bed of the lorry

C It will create an environmental hazard

D It will react with the asphalt, creating explosive fumes

19.03

When kerbing works are being carried out, how should kerbs be taken off the vehicle?

A Lift them off manually using the correct technique

B Push them off the back

C Use mechanical means, such as a machine fitted with a grab

D Ask your workmate to give you a hand

19.04

What are **two** effects of under-inflated tyres on the operation of a machine?

A It decreases the operating speed of the engine

B It can make the machine unstable

C It causes increased tyre wear

D It decreases tyre wear

E It increases the operating speed of the engine

19.05

Which of the following is true in relation to the safe working load of lifting equipment, such as a cherry picker, lorry loader or excavator?

A It must never be exceeded

B It is a guide figure that may be exceeded slightly

C It may be exceeded by 10% only

D It gives half the maximum weight to be lifted

F
19

19.06

Which checks should the operator of a mobile elevating work platform (MEWP), for example a cherry picker, carry out before using it?

A That a seat belt is provided for the operator

B That a roll-over cage is fitted

C That the hydraulic system is drained

D That emergency systems operate correctly

19.07

In which of the following circumstances would it **not** be safe to use a cherry picker for working at height?

A When a roll-over cage is not fitted

B When the ground is uneven and sloping

C When weather protection is not fitted

D When the operator is clipped to an anchorage point in the basket

19.08

A single vehicle is carrying out mobile highway works during the day. What **must** be clearly displayed on or at the rear of the vehicle?

A A road narrows (left or right) sign

B A specific task warning sign (for example, gully cleaning)

C A keep left or right arrow

D A roadworks ahead sign

19.09

What action is required when a highways vehicle fitted with a direction arrow is travelling from site to site?

A Point the direction arrow up

B Travel slowly from site to site

C Point the direction arrow down

D Cover or remove the direction arrow

19.10

When should the amber flashing beacon fitted to a highways vehicle be switched on?

A At all times

B When travelling to and from the depot

C When the vehicle is being used as a works vehicle

D Only in poor visibility

19.11

How often must a competent person thoroughly examine lifting equipment for lifting persons, for example a cherry picker?

A Every 6 months

B Every 12 months

C Every 18 months

D Every 24 months

F

19

19.12

When undertaking a site survey on a dual carriageway with a 60 mph speed limit what is the minimum standard of hi-vis clothing that **must** be worn?

- A Reflective waistcoat
- B Reflective long-sleeved jacket
- C Reflective sash
- D None

19.13

Why is it necessary to wear hi-vis clothing when working on roads?

- A So road users and plant operators can see you
- B So that your colleagues can see you
- C To protect the clothes underneath from damage
- D Because it will keep you warm

19.14

When providing portable traffic signals on minor rural roads used by cyclists, what action should be taken by the contractor?

- A Locate the signals at bends in the road
- B Allow more time for slow-moving traffic by increasing the 'all red' phase of the signals
- C Operate the signals manually
- D Use stop and go boards only

19.15

What is the main reason why temporary highways signing needs to be removed when works are completed?

- A To get traffic flowing
- B It is a legal requirement
- C To allow the road to be opened fully
- D To reuse signs on new jobs

19.16

When should installed highways signs and guarding equipment be inspected?

- A Immediately after it has been used
- B No more frequently than once a week
- C Every hour, except when the site is unattended
- D Regularly and at least once every day, including when the site is unattended

19.17

How **must** signs on footways be located?

- A So that they block the footway
- B So that they can be read by site personnel
- C So that they do not create a hazard for pedestrians
- D So that they can be easily removed

F
19

19.18

What should the contractor do when drivers who are approaching roadworks cannot easily see any advance roadwork signs because of poor visibility or other obstructions?

A Place additional signs in advance of the works

B Extend the safety zones

C Extend the sideways clearance

D Lengthen the lead-in taper

19.19

What action is required where passing traffic may block the view of highways signs?

A Signs must be larger

B Signs must be duplicated on both sides of the road

C Signs must be placed higher

D A flashing light placed on top of the sign

19.20

In which **two** places would you find information about the distances for setting out highways signs in advance of the works under different road conditions?

A In the Traffic Signs Manual (Chapter 8)

B In the Pink Book

C On the back of the sign

D In the Works Order

E In the new Code of Practice (Red Book)

19.21

How must highways signs, lights and guarding equipment be properly secured?

A With built-in weights where possible

B By roping them to concrete blocks or kerb stones

C To prevent them being stolen

D By iron weights suspended from the frame by chains or other strong material

19.22

When working after dark, is mobile plant exempt from the requirement to show lights?

A Yes, always

B Yes, if authorised by the supervisor

C Only if they are not fitted to the machine as standard

D Not in any circumstances

F
19

Answers: 19.18 = A   19.19 = B   19.20 = A, E   19.21 = A   19.22 = D

Further information

Contents

Preparing for the case studies

Construction is an exciting industry. There is constant change as work progresses to completion.

As a result, the construction site is one of the most dangerous environments to work in.

Everyone on site working together can avoid many of the accidents that happen. The free film *Setting out* shows what you and the site must do to stay healthy and safe at work.

To watch the film:

 go online at *www.citb.co.uk/settingout.*

This film is essential viewing for everyone involved in construction, and should be viewed before sitting the CITB *Health, safety and environment test.*

The content of the film is summarised here. These principles form the basis for the behavioural case studies.

It is advisable to watch the film. However, for those unable to view it or who want to refresh themselves on the content, the full transcript is provided for your information.

Part 1: What you should expect from the construction industry

Your site and your employer should be doing all they can to keep you and your colleagues safe.

Before any work begins, the site management team will have been planning and preparing the site for your arrival. It's their job to ensure that you can do your job safely and efficiently.

Five things the site you are working on must do:

- ☑ know when you are on site
- ☑ give you a site induction
- ☑ give you site-specific information
- ☑ encourage communication
- ☑ keep you up to date and informed.

Part 2: What the industry expects of you

Once the work begins, it's up to every individual to take responsibility for carrying out the plan safely.

This means you should follow the rules and guidelines as well as being alert to the continuing changes on site.

Five things you must do:

- ☑ respect and follow the site rules
- ☑ safely prepare each task
- ☑ carry out each task responsibly
- ☑ know when to stop (if you think anything is unsafe)
- ☑ keep learning.

Setting out – the transcript

What to expect from the industry and what the industry expects from you

Construction is an exciting industry. There is constant change as work progresses to completion.

As a result, the construction site is one of the most dangerous environments to work in.

Many accidents that occur on sites can be avoided. In this film you will find out what you and the site must do to stay healthy and safe at work.

Part 1: What to expect from the industry

When you arrive for your first day on a site, it will not be the first day for everyone.

Before any work begins, the site management team will have been planning and preparing the site for your arrival.

It is *their* job to ensure that you can do *your* job safely and efficiently.

So what are five key things the site should do for you?

1. Your site must know when you are on site

When you arrive you should be greeted and welcomed by someone on site. If you are not then make your presence known to site management.

You need to know who is in charge and they need to know who is working on, or visiting, their site.

You may be asked to sign in or report to someone in charge when you arrive. You should also sign out or let someone know if you are leaving.

2. Your site must give you an induction

Once you have introduced yourself, you will be given a site induction. This is a legal requirement to give you basic information so that you can work safely on site.

You may be asked to watch a video or look at a presentation. It is important that you understand what is said during the induction. If there is something you are not sure about, don't be afraid to ask for more information. If you have not been to the site for a while, you need to be sure that you are up to date. Check with site management whether you need a briefing or a further induction.

3. Your site must give you site-specific information

Whether you are just starting out or have decades of experience, every job is different. So it is very important that the site induction is specific to your site.

You should be told about any specific areas of danger and what site rules are in place to control these.

You will be told who the managers are on site and what arrangements are in place for emergencies.

You will also find out what to do it there is a fire or if you need to sound an alarm.

It may sound basic, but there must be good welfare facilities.

You must also be able to take a break somewhere that is warm and dry.

4. Your site must encourage communication

Evidence shows that there are fewer incidents and accidents on sites where workers are actively involved in health and safety. Your opinions and ideas are important so make them heard.

Whatever the size of your site there should be many opportunities to do this. For example, directly with managers through a daily briefing or through suggestion boxes. Managers should let you know how best to do this on your site.

5. Your site must keep you up to date

Construction sites are constantly changing and unplanned activities can be a major cause of accidents. The more up to date you are about what is happening on site, the more you can understand the dangers. The best sites keep their people informed on daily activities.

Is there a hazards board on your site – is it regularly updated?

Your site management should be telling you what's going on, on a regular basis.

Your site should be doing all it can to keep you and your colleagues safe. If it is not – say something and work together to make it better.

Part 2: What the industry expects from you

Site management will have planned ahead to make work on site as safe as possible for you. Once the work begins, it is up to every individual to take responsibility for carrying out the plan safely. This means following the guidelines set out and being alert to the continuing changes on site.

So what will the site expect from you?

1. You must respect site rules

Site rules are there to minimise the risk of particularly hazardous activities, such as moving vehicles and handling flammable substances.

Moving traffic on site is a major cause of accidents. Often rules will cover issues like walking through the site, where to park, and how to behave when you see a moving vehicle.

They may also tell you where you can smoke and remind you to tidy equipment away when it is not in use.

These might feel restrictive but they have been put in place for a reason. If that reason is not clear to you, ask for more information. Otherwise, follow the rules to stay safe.

2. You must safely prepare each task

Every task carried out on site is unique and will have its own dangers, for instance working at height or manual handling. The site management team will put in place a plan to avoid or minimise the dangers before the start of work. The plan may be written down in a risk assessment, a method statement or a task sheet.

This will tell you what to do, the skills needed, what to wear, what tools to use and what the dangers are.

You should contribute to the planning process using your experience and knowledge.

For example, before working at height, which is a high-risk activity, you must consider:

- ☑ Is the access suitable for what you need to do?
- ☑ Do you have the right tools?
- ☑ Do you have the right protective equipment, does it fit, and is it comfortable?

3. You must do each task responsibly

Once you are at work you must apply your training, skills and common sense to your tasks at all times.

For example, if you are building a wall, you may have to move heavy loads. But you must not put your health and body in danger. Make sure you move the load as safely as possible, as you should have been trained to do. And if you are not sure how to, then you must ask for advice.

Equally, it is important to be aware of the dangers to those around you. For example, if someone working with you is not wearing the correct PPE for a certain activity, tell them so.

Acting responsibly will benefit both you and your colleagues.

4. You must know when to stop

In our industry saying NO is not easy. We are fixers and doers. We CAN do.

However, a significant number of accidents on sites happen when people are doing things that they're not comfortable with.

For example, many workers have been harmed by not knowing how to identify asbestos. If you think there is any likelihood that there is asbestos present where you are working, you must stop work and seek advice.

If you are not properly trained, equipped, or briefed – or if the situation around you changes – the result could be an accident.

Trust your instincts. If things feel beyond your control or dangerous or, if you see someone else working unsafely, stop the work immediately and inform site management why you have done so.

You might prevent an injury or save a life. Your employer should be supportive if you do this because you have the right to say no and the responsibility to not walk by.

5. You must keep learning

If your job requires you to have specific training to enable you to do it safely then it is your employer's responsibility to provide it.

To really get the best out of your career, you should keep learning about developments in machinery, equipment, regulations and training.

This will not only give you greater confidence and understanding, it will ensure you remain healthy and safe.

In summary

Construction is so much more than bricks and mortar. The work we do improves the world around us. It's time for us to work together to build a safer and better industry.